THE GROCER'S BOY GETS DOWN TO BUSINESS

ROBERT MURRAY

Other Books by
Robert Murray

The Grocer's Boy:
A Slice of His Life in 1950s Scotland

The Spirit of Robbie Burns

The Grocer's Boy Rides Again:
Another Slice of His Life in
1960s Scotland and Beyond

THE GROCER'S BOY GETS DOWN TO BUSINESS

The End Slice of His Career from the Easy-Going Seventies to the Ultra-Competitive Nineties

Robert Murray

The Grocer's Boy Gets Down to Business: The End Slice of His Career from the Easy-Going Seventies to the Ultra-Competitive Nineties by Robert Murray.

First published in Great Britain in 2022 by Extremis Publishing Ltd.,
Suite 218, Castle House, 1 Baker Street, Stirling, FK8 1AL, United Kingdom.
www.extremispublishing.com

Extremis Publishing is a Private Limited Company registered in Scotland (SC509983) whose Registered Office is Suite 218, Castle House, 1 Baker Street, Stirling, FK8 1AL, United Kingdom.

A CIP catalogue record for this book is available from the British Library.

ISBN: 978-1-7398543-2-4

Typeset in Goudy Bookletter 1911, designed by The League of Moveable Type.

Printed and bound in Great Britain by IngramSpark, Chapter House, Pitfield, Kiln Farm, Milton Keynes, MK11 3LW, United Kingdom.

Depot Locations (Excluding Retail Stores)

At December 31, 1992

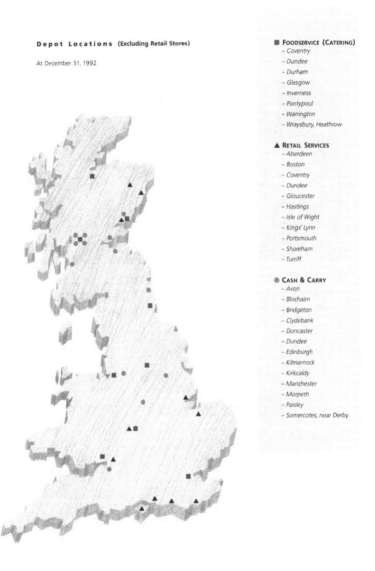

■ FOODSERVICE (CATERING)
– Coventry
– Dundee
– Durham
– Glasgow
– Inverness
– Pontypool
– Warrington
– Wraysbury, Heathrow

▲ RETAIL SERVICES
– Aberdeen
– Boston
– Coventry
– Dundee
– Gloucester
– Hastings
– Isle of Wight
– Kings' Lynn
– Portsmouth
– Shoreham
– Turriff

● CASH & CARRY
– Avon
– Blochairn
– Bridgeton
– Clydebank
– Doncaster
– Dundee
– Edinburgh
– Kilmarnock
– Kirkcaldy
– Manchester
– Morpeth
– Paisley
– Somercotes, near Derby

Locations of Watson and Philip Distribution Centres, December 1992

The Watson and Philip board of directors, circa the 1970s,
featuring Herbert Philip (left), J.B. Thomson (centre),
Frank Philip (right) and Harry Gardner (far right).

The Watson and Philip board of directors in the early
1990s, with chief executive Ian Macpherson (centre).

THE GROCER'S BOY GETS DOWN TO BUSINESS

The End Slice of His Career from the Easy-Going Seventies to the Ultra-Competitive Nineties

Robert Murray

PREFACE

I N 1953, the year of our Queen Elizabeth's coronation, I commenced work with Wm Low & Co Ltd as a twelve year old retail grocery 'message boy' delivering 'orders' in and around my home town of Carnoustie – a small seaside holiday resort on the east coast of Scotland. The food trade, with its energy and connection with people in the days of 'counter-service' shops, captured my interest and imagination, and I commenced my apprenticeship when I was fifteen years old. By the time I celebrated my 23rd birthday, I had managed three of the company's branches – all in the city of Dundee, some twelve miles away from my home.

My seemingly irrational decision in 1963 to leave the company and join Dundee Commercial College as a lecturer in distributive trades subjects proved, miraculously, to have been a helpful 'stepping stone' when, in 1968, I joined the London-based Grocers' Institute as a Training Development Officer. My combined work experiences led me in December 1969 to join the Dundee-based wholesale food distributor Watson and Philip Ltd (W&P) as the company's first training officer.

This story reflects my 33 years of working for that well-known and respected organisation which, over those years, became a major player in the burgeoning and technically advancing UK wholesale and retail food industry.

My good fortune was to be part of that journey, as was the opportunity to work with the talented and experienced people around me. From the moment I stepped into W&P I immediately sensed the friendly, hard-working team spirit – it fitted me like a long-lost glove. In those days, the word 'career' never entered my vocabulary or those of my colleagues – all we shared was a strong identity and a superb work ethic.

My story reflects successive family generations of corporate skill, innovation, enterprise, ambition and rewarding successes – all of which, alas, ended in tragedy.

This third book in *The Grocer's Boy* series is about the development of the highly respected W&P, its growth in the retail and wholesale food industry in the UK from 1969, and my story in it until the company's disastrous demise in 2002.

CHAPTER 1

January 1970: "Another Baby Expected!", or "Learning About the Business and People"

L ONDON, Cambridge, The Grocers' Institute and my experiences as a Training Development Officer driving around colleges and businesses in my 'patch', from the Thames to the Humber and east of the M1 motorway, were all behind me now, and another chapter in my working life beckoned.

It was a Friday evening in January, and I'd earlier enjoyed my favourites – mum's special homemade broth and her tasty steak pie with mum, dad, and my sisters Isobel and Jean. My brother Peem (a nickname for some boys called James on the east coast of Scotland) and I were catching up on our news while sitting in The Station Hotel pub in Carnoustie.

During several weeks in late 1969 I had carried out, at the request of Divisional Managing Director, Harry Gardner, an initial assessment of training needs for my new employer, the Delivered Grocery Division of Watson & Philip plc. Thereafter, I'd spent Christmas and New Year in St Ives (near Cambridge) with my wife and three-year old daughter Carys, and this was my first opportunity for some time to chat with my brother.

"Well, Robbie, you've been back from England for a week now," Peem said with a smile. "What's your news?"

"It's going well, Peem. Just beginning to meet my new colleagues and find out how the business runs. In fact, I had a humorous start with one of the senior managers."

"That sounds like a good beginning."

"Well, luckily it ended happily, but I think I gave him a shock," I admitted.

My brother looked slightly alarmed. "Tell me more," he prompted me.

"It was the start of my induction at the company's headquarters at Blackness Road in Dundee. I decided to have a chat with Eddie Thompson, the Operations Manager for the Delivered Grocery Division.

"I was standing outside his ground floor office and could see, through a large glass wall, he was sitting at his desk and only partially viewable behind a high stack of document trays, and his secretary was writing in her shorthand note-book while he was dictating something.

"Eddie motioned me to enter and have a seat. He was concluding his dictation: '...and I am extremely sorry that you found a cigarette end within the roll of streaky bacon. My sincere apologies, and I can assure you this will never happen

4

"My sincere apologies... I can assure you this will never happen again!"

again. I will arrange a discount on your next invoice. Thanking you for your continued custom, yours faithfully...'

"Eddie then thanked Anne, and asked her to make sure the letter would be dispatched that evening. His secretary left, and Eddie stood up to shake hands. 'Hello Bob, and a Happy New Year to you. How are you doing?' he asked.

"'Happy New Year, Eddie!' I replied. 'I'm fine, thanks. that's a very novel way to smoke your bacon these days! Are you saving on fuel'?"

I explained to Peem: "Eddie, a qualified CA and originally from Glasgow, sat stunned for a moment, and I thought he was going to react badly. His face reddened, but then beamed as he smiled widely and joked: 'Yes, it's our way of showing we smoke each piece individually to order'."

"That wasn't like you, Robbie, to make such a bold statement," Peem remarked.

"You're right, Peem. But I had previously felt an immediate rapport with Eddie when I discovered we both had an account with Collars Ltd. in Glasgow."

"What do you mean?" he asked, looking confused.

"Collars, Glasgow, sent to me on a regular basis; a box of perfectly laundered and starched collars. Using a stud, I could fix on a clean collar every day and wear the same shirt for a few days. After a month or so I'd send the used collars back to the company for cleaning and re-starching." Peem, the artist, seemed bemused. Such a creative person didn't have to think of such boring subjects as starched collars.

Looking back, it sounds rather a lazy practice, but when the children were young it saved busy housewives washing shirts every day. In times when washing machines and tumble dryers were in their infancy, immaculate collars from Glasgow were useful for everyday workwear. It wasn't an important matter, but in a rather strange way it indicated that Eddie and I were somehow on the same kind of odd wavelength.

"When I think of it, Peem, he was prepared to allow me to overhear his dictation. He could have avoided that if he had wanted to. Although Eddie's face was flushed, I realised it was only his form of slight embarrassment. I could tell from our previous chats that he was a shrewd and efficient man – and, I guessed, about the same age as myself."

Peem and I continued our chat. He brought me up to date with events in Carnoustie and about his work progress in DC Thomson, the newspaper and publishing company, where he was employed as an artist.

It was a great pity that Mum and Dad couldn't accommodate me, but all the bedrooms at home were occupied. All too soon I had to set off on my fifteen-mile drive to my in-laws in Kirriemuir, and Peem and I parted with a plan to keep in regular touch.

As I drove, I thought back on my first week as an employee in the company. My encounter with Eddie preoccupied my thoughts.

* * *

I had met Eddie during my training needs analysis several weeks before Christmas and knew that he was responsible for warehouse, transport, the bacon department and the division's office functions. He had given me a detailed account of his part in the business. His jocular reply indicated his sense of humour, and I realised I had created a good rapport with him.

We chatted briefly, and I learned he had joined W&P less than two years previously. I outlined my initial programme to meet all of the directors and managers.

"When are you going to tell me what training I need?" Eddie had asked me with an impish grin.

"Oh, I'll need to switch on the bright lamp on my desk and interrogate you," I told him.

"No, just use the lamp on my desk," he offered in reply. It was a clever, humorous and yet assertive response. We each laughed, but I knew Eddie was not to be taken too lightly.

I thanked him for his time and, before leaving, he added: "By the way, Bob – when you get a chance, let me know your thoughts after you visit the bacon department." I took the point!

A queue had formed outside Eddie's office and I quickly realised he was pressed for time, so I made my exit. I had noticed that invariably there was almost always a queue of staff waiting to speak with him; he was an important, key figure in the business.

My thoughts returned to the conversation with my brother. "When I sell the property in St Ives, in Huntington," I'd told him, "I'll be able to move back here – and meanwhile I'll have a look around for a house. It's a shame Gail and Carys are left there," by which I was referring to my wife and young daughter, "but Carys is happy attending a playgroup in the town and there's a plan to possibly bring them here at Easter. However, there's more good news."

"Oh? What's that?" Peem had enquired with his usual fraternal curiosity and concern.

"We're expecting an addition to the family! Yes, there's a new baby due around July sometime. So I must be organised with a new home in Dundee by then. In the meantime, my in-laws at Kirriemuir have offered to accommodate me."

As I continued to drive, I considered all that I had learned during that first week as an employee. During December, I had earlier agreed my induction programme within the company with my boss, Harry Gardner, and for the next two weeks I'd hardly be in my office as I moved around the business. My initial intention was to meet all of the managers within the division, and thereafter meet the directors of each division of the company. Apart from the Chairman, Mr Herbert Philip, all directors were based at the corporate headquarters at Blackness Road.

First and foremost, I had to be aware that I was a 'new animal' – a rare beast: a Training Officer – and I had to realise, as my boss had indicated, that I may be regarded with some suspicion and scepticism. I knew this meant I had to 'sell' myself sensibly.

This is a critical stage, Robbie Murray – one of the most sensitive in your working life so far. It's important to be down to earth, practical and supportive.

The company, I had been informed, was a long established one, having been created in 1873 by two partners named Thomas Watson and Joseph Philip. Over the years, the business had progressed from being a supplier of foodstuffs to the catering trade and, in January 1968, had been formed into four divisions with a central administration function supporting the four profit-making sectors.

My appointment, commencing 1st December 1969, was as Training Officer within one division – namely 'Delivered Grocery' – and although I had spent valuable time with each manager in November while I conducted a training survey, it had been as an 'external adviser' and not as an employee. Consequently, my priority now was to meet with each department head, as a colleague, and refer to the training plan as identified during my earlier discussions.

Having visited Eddie, my next arranged visit was to the office of the Sales Manager, Alastair, who explained that his customers were owners of retail grocery businesses spread across Scotland. There were two categories: those who were 'signed up' as members of the UK-wide Voluntary Group called VG, and those who ran smaller shops and felt they did not require the 'backing' of advertising, operational advice, sales promotions and a national identity. Such smaller shops were labelled 'Pinnacle', which was an old product name within the company.

VG retailers were required to sign an agreement to follow the rules of the franchise and pay a weekly charge for the services they received, such as in-store marketing material which linked with radio, television and newspaper advertising. In addition, they paid a surcharge on the goods they purchased: the more they bought, the less the charge. Benefits were significant – national branding by a range of 'own brand' products, shop front fascia board, free store layouts and updated legal advice.

As Sales Manager, Alastair's function was to oversee consultants who were ensuring that franchise rules for retailers were being correctly applied. He had five male VG sales consultants reporting to him. Each had a territory base in Scotland and supervised the retailers, and they advised them on every means by which they could improve business – hence the word 'consultant' rather than 'salesman'. The UK was divided into VG territories roughly delineated by the various commercial TV company advertising areas. The practice behind this was that within each TV area was a dedicated wholesale company which operated the VG franchise, and in Scotland that was Watson and Philip plc.

Alastair, a progressive thinker, had previously informed me he had two training priorities: firstly, to train his consultants on how to better develop business, and secondly, to train his consultants and over 200 VG retailers in Scotland on the forthcoming needs to cope with UK government plans to implement decimalisation in the February of 1971.

We agreed a date and time to meet and discuss his training ambitions in more detail. "It's great timing that you're here, Bob," he told me. "We certainly have a need for help."

"That's good to know, Alastair. I'm sure Harry Gardner had those ideas in mind when he told you he was looking for a training officer," I observed.

"Yes, that was a well-timed phone call to me, Bob." He was referring to the evening the previous September when I had called Alastair from England to ask if the rumour that the company was seeking a training officer (I had amazingly heard about in a London pub) was true. He had been instrumental in passing on my interest to his boss, Harry.

Alastair, I could sense, was relieved that training help had arrived and genuinely pleased to have been involved in my eventual appointment. As I left our meeting, I felt a shared desire to get on with his creative training aspirations. He needed no converting!

Okay, Murray, two meetings – both sound good so far. Where to next? Ah, yes – the warehouse!

I'd been told the entire office block and warehouse area had been, since the late 19th century, a long-standing and important foundry in the city. W&P had previously operated in cramped accommodation in the city's harbour area at Esplanade Buildings on the corner of Union Street and Craig Street, and now had the luxury of space to expand the business. In recent years, the company had gradually adapted this larger space to suit its needs for the other divisions within the company.

As I walked down the steel staircase into the warehouse, two floor levels below, I paused and took in the view of the 60,000 square foot floor area of the warehouse. It was not far short of the dimension of a football pitch. The floor space was entirely taken up with long rows of high racking framework, into which there were spaces where a loaded pallet could be slotted. Thus, with five or six loaded pallets piled vertically, the racking was approximately thirty or forty feet high.

Douglas, the warehouse and transport manager, was engaged in a conversation with an employee, so I took my time to look around. Like Eddie and Alastair, I had previously spent time speaking with Douglas when I conducted my initial training analysis.

Soon he was free to speak. "Hello, Bob," he said with a smile. "So you're one of us now?"

"Hi, Douglas. Yes, that's right – for better or for worse. I'm looking forward to it."

"What do you want to speak about?"

"Well, I'd like to learn a lot more about how you operate here, Douglas. All about your warehouse world."

"Okay then, let's have a walk around," he suggested. "We'll go to 'goods-in', then follow the route of the goods."

On the way I asked him an obvious question. "Are all of your products food?"

"No, we sell cigarettes, spirits and some non-foods such as kitchen and toilet cleansers and paper products, but it's mainly bottles, packets and canned products. Everything arrives on pallets and is picked up here at 'goods-in' by forklift trucks and taken to its allotted space. The pallets on the floor of the racking, and those on the first level of racking, are what we call 'picking-lines'. That means the order pickers assemble customers' orders from those levels. All the pallets on levels above... those are what we call bulk storage. In other words, stock that is ready in due course to be brought down to be picked. The topmost pallets being so high means that special high-reach forklift trucks capable of putting loaded pallets at least thirty feet high are needed."

Remembering my Willie Low retail days, I asked him: "How do you ensure proper stock rotation?"

"Ah, that's easy," he replied. "Every pallet that comes in is logged on a 'Visapost' system, which keeps a record of the date and where that pallet is stored."

"Is it a computer system?"

"No, we're not that advanced. It's a manual card index system."

"So every slot has a reference?"

"Yes, every line of racking and each level is labelled."

I had a quick look around and counted around ten lines of racking – each about forty yards long – occupying a central space of the warehouse floor area. The whole area had wide aisles around it, and a further ten shorter lines of equally high racking down one side of the warehouse.

"So, Douglas," I enquired, "you have fork lift operators who take stock from goods-in to the bulk racks, and presumably they also have the job to bring down pallets into the picking line too?"

"That's right," he told me.

"And your other group of workers are the pickers?"

"Yes, they use a 'unitainer' – we call them cages – into which the goods are packed and then assembled at the loading bay, ready to be put on lorries at the loading bank," he explained. "The cages go on the vehicle and are dropped down at the shops by means of a hydraulic tail-lift."

"And what does that long chain inset into the warehouse floor do?"

"Good question! When this warehouse was set up a few years ago, the consultants installed a thing called an Acrow cart system."

I was genuinely intrigued. "How did that work?"

"Well, the chain you see in the floor – with slots at various intervals – moved around the warehouse at a predetermined speed, and it meant that a picker could 'unhitch' from it a moving cart with a cage on it so they didn't have to walk to the loading bay to pick up an empty cage on a cart. Likewise, when they had filled a cage, they put the cart with the filled cage back into the chain and somebody at the loading bay would unhitch it and arrange the cages in an orderly queue ready to be loaded onto lorries. It was a work-study based system."

"Why are you not using it now?" I asked him.

"The carts were ungainly to move about, but – more importantly – it was dangerous. If something was in the way of the cart as it moved around then it couldn't be stopped quickly, and there were cases where there were 'pile-ups' which resulted in the racking being damaged – and potentially pallets could fall out of the racking. We had one case where an inexperienced picker was trapped between a moving cart and the racking, and ended up with a broken leg."

This was all valuable information about how the warehouse operations worked. "Okay, so you have forklift guys and pickers – what else do you have?"

"I have one man on the 'Visapost', four forklift men, twelve order-pickers, and usually nearer the end of the day I switch some fellas onto loading filled cages on to lorries. Of course, I have fifteen lorry drivers too."

"What problems or issues do you have then Douglas?" I queried.

Thoughtfully, he replied, "Like I said when you did your analysis, my biggest problem is goods being damaged in the cages during transit to shops. They come back as damaged goods, and it's lost stock. Eddie's not happy with that."

"What's the cause of that?"

"Cages badly packed by the pickers," he told me. "By that I mean putting light or weak boxes or packages on the bottom of the cage and heavy items on top. It causes broken bottles, and damage to other stock. I need help to train forklift men and to train pickers to pack properly."

"What about the lorry drivers?" I wondered.

"Not a problem. They're all qualified – but like everything else, there are good drivers and some not so good."

By now we had spent valuable time examining each aspect in some detail, and time was wearing on. I glanced at my watch. "Look, Douglas; it's lunch time. I should let you get home."

"No, it's okay," he told me. "I eat in the canteen."

"I will too."

As we walked up the steel staircase, which took us past the door of Eddie's office, I thanked Douglas for his time and we agreed to speak sometime later about arranging a date for training his pickers and forklift men.

Good start then, Robbie – training for sales consultants, retailers, forklift drivers and order-pickers. Time to plan ahead. The bacon and printing departments, the office, and then the heavy goods vehicle workshops to visit this afternoon.

CHAPTER 2

"Lunchtime Chat", or "Expectations and Influence"

THE four-floor office block was of late 19th century appearance and, although there was a centrally located spiral staircase that linked each floor to the top of the building, there was also a 'maximum four person' lift with a folding steel 'gate'.

Douglas pressed the button and, with some clanking noises, the lift-gate appeared behind the small window in the concertina outer door. "It makes some weird noises, but it hasn't let anyone down yet," he joked.

I hoped he was right, but soon – despite background creaking and clanging noises – we were safely and efficiently conveyed to the canteen floor at the top of the building. As we emerged, I could see immediately in front of me the framework of what appeared to be a new office wall. John the 'handyman' was busy cutting a large piece of plywood.

"It's coming on well, Bob," Douglas remarked as we passed by.

"Yes, you're right – it'll soon be ready for action," I smiled in response.

My reply, I hoped, had sounded confident. The new 'office' was in fact the planned training room which my boss Harry Gardner had designed and commissioned to be built by John Devine, the talented aforementioned in-house handyman/technician/tradesman. Harry had outlined to me his plans when I had worked on the training analysis the previous November. Now the reality was taking shape, and I looked forward to the as-yet-unknown training activity. I was becoming increasingly aware of Harry's expectations, and of course the influence I was expected to bring. Douglas's remark indicated that Harry had informed the management team of his training plans.

Harry's plan included a red lightbulb which would be switched on when training was in progress, and was fixed to the outside of the wall near the door to avoid interruptions. I'd queried this idea with Harry when he joked about having the only 'red light district' in Dundee. "It'll be a Devine training room all for you, Robert!" Harry had teased.

Two ladies worked in a kitchen – which was presumably designed, built and fitted out by the versatile joiner John – and long tables (only long tables – no two or four seaters) were spaced out in a comfortable and spacious dining area. I'd eaten in the canteen during my earlier 'fact-finding' visit, and recognised some of the faces.

I guessed Harry had planned the long tables – he obviously wanted to avoid 'cliques', and wished to promote mixing. It seemed to work, as I found myself sitting with Douglas, John – an office manager – a VG sales consultant and office clerk named Gordon, and Bill the bacon manager. The conversation was wide and varied: everything from world and sporting news to Dundee events, but nothing about people or happenings within the company. The impression was that there was to be no 'office gossip'. I was made to feel welcome, and I quickly felt at ease in the friendly, jocular environment.

Surprisingly, Eddie turned up later just as we were finishing our cups of tea, and the chat continued. I learned on that first day a good deal of teasing dominated when it came to football successes and failures, with Rangers obviously Eddie's favourite and Dundee United seemingly Douglas's. Although I'd lost the up-to-date Scottish football news during my recent two years spent in England, it was all entertaining fun and I made a determined mental note to try and keep up to date with the football news.

Bill the bacon manager was first to stand up. "I must get on. I've got smoking to do this afternoon," he told us. I could have, but didn't, say "See you later," as I instinctively felt there was an unwritten rule: "Don't discuss what work you're doing, or with whom, at the lunch table."

My eye caught Eddie's amused face at Bill's 'smoking' comment, but nothing was said. It summed up lunchtimes: they were for relaxation, and work was not to be discussed.

Harry's influence seemed to be all around me – the training room, canteen layout, and my very presence in the company. It was clear he was bringing with him some professional touches from his previous management experience within the VG grocery business in the London region.

At long last, Murray – colleagues to sit and chat with on a daily basis. Something you've never had in your working life. Enjoy it!

* * *

My afternoon began with a ground floor visit to the printing department, which was housed in an area roughly the size of half a badminton court. Another Douglas – an older man – was in charge here, and worked with one assistant.

This was my first meeting with him, and he told me his work was almost entirely devoted to printing promotional leaflets and shop window bills for use by retailers. This was part of what VG retailers were paying for – that is, anything which helped to promote sales. His other major piece of work, he told me, was to print PLOF's.

"What's a PLOF, Douglas?" I asked with genuine curiosity.

"It's the Price List Order Form," he informed me.

"That must be an important item to print!"

"Aye, and there's big pressure with it," he said, wiping his forehead.

"Why is that?"

He picked up a wad of probably fifteen or twenty A4 double-sided printed pages, stapled together, and opened up at a page to explain.

"The PLOF is the customer's order form, listing every item we stock. You'll see, for example, on this page each product is listed with size, description and price, along with a space for the customer to enter how many boxes or packs are required. A blank PLOF for the next order goes out with every completed order, and by a certain date the customer posts it back with requirements marked and attaches a cheque for the previous order. The order does not get picked unless the cheque clears"

"Yes, I saw the order pickers in the warehouse using the PLOF which tells them what to pick."

He nodded in approval at my observation. "So there's always pressure to make sure the new PLOF is printed in time to go out with an order."

"I see. And what happens to the posters and leaflets?"

"Well, all the new updated material has to be ready to go out with the order too."

"Timing is important then, Douglas?"

"Oh yes," he agreed. "I must get the price changes from the Buying Department on time to print them in the PLOF, and I dare not hold up the new PLOFs which must go with the order."

For the full duration of our chat, we had to speak over the noise of his printing off-set lithograph machines. Douglas's work seemed to be one of a constant cycle, with little room for delay. He oversaw the typesetting and running, and his assistant had the job of collating packs of advertising material and PLOF's for each retailer. In terms of training, there seemed to be nothing for me to contemplate.

"Do you have any problems here then, Douglas?" I prompted him.

He thought about my question. "Just waiting for price changes and leaflets and poster information to come in good time to me from the buyers," he told me.

It was immediately obvious: here was a vital part of the business run by one man and an assistant, entirely dependent on the efficiency and coordination of other departments. He had to get information in as well as meet deadlines to get his product out.

"And is your assistant able to stand in for you, Douglas?"

"Oh yes, when I go on holiday," he reassured me. Despite the constant pressure, Douglas appeared to have things well in hand.

Our meeting was conducted at an unsuitable time and situation, but I was now far better informed and fortunately had seen the operation in action. "Thanks, Douglas, for your time. I wish you a smooth week ahead."

"Aye, but I've forgotten to tell you – I have to do the same for all the Pinnacle customers too, without the advertising."

As I walked away, I realised how critical his part was in the operation. Now, I could see how Alastair's customers were provided with the help they were paying for. What I forgot to ask Douglas was how the customer then received an invoice for the goods picked. I made a mental note to enquire with someone in the office. My only other observation was that Douglas was a man apparently approaching retirement age. A recruitment issue someday, perhaps? And was the assistant capable of standing in long term? An answer would be required at some point.

No immediate training needs there, Robbie... but sometime, ask Harry about succession planning for Douglas.

* * *

When I left printing, I realised I was quite close to the vehicle workshop. Since I had not been able to obtain a precise time to meet Frank, the foreman mechanic, I took the opportunity to go down a back stairway to street level and say hello.

Once again, here was a man with deadlines and – ever aware of the need not to distract people – I conducted most of my chat while Frank was on his back under a VG delivery truck.

"What's your main job, Frank?" I asked him politely, keen to understand more about what went on here.

"A' thing and everything," he told me matter-of-factly.

"I'm sure. What are the main repairs you do?"

"Just making sure the servicing of the trucks is done. That means oil changes, tyres and brakes, and any repairs to damage like lights."

Clearly this was all important work. "How many vehicles do you have to service?" I enquired.

"About fifteen. Plus, the bacon vans."

"Anything else?"

"Well, a bit of welding work in the warehouse sometimes," he said.

Frank was obviously a busy man, and had the ability to turn his skills to good effect. He worked alone and obviously had to make his own decisions about his time management.

There seemed no point in distracting Frank for – as with Douglas, the printer – it was important to let them get on with the job. In each case I saw no need for training, although – looking back – I think there were probably Health and Safety issues to be considered for both employees, especially when working alone. But safety was not so high up on the agenda in those days.

"Good to meet you, Frank," I told him as I departed.

"And you, Mr Murray," he said in response.

I became aware of the need to take care not to give employees any impressions that I had been sent to speak with them because they needed training.

Like printing, there was no need for training here as both individuals were well on top of the job (or, in Frank's case, well under it). The only potential problem would be replacing staff if and when it ever became necessary.

My next planned visit was to meet Bill, the bacon processing manager. This was of particular interest for me since I had good bacon experience within a retail context, but this was a process I hadn't witnessed.

Bill, I found, was an industrious man with a genuine desire to run his processing unit efficiently. His department was housed in a corner of the warehouse, near to the loading bay. In fact, he had a section of the loading bay for his own departmental use.

"What goes on here, Bill?"

The smiling, bespectacled and slightly-built man was ready with his answers. "Our main function is to buy in bacon – backs, shoulders, hams and streaky. We bone the shoulders and hams, as well as boil hams, and seal them in viscose wrap.[1] We also 'bone out' and smoke the streaky and backs."

There were five or six employees of varying ages and all seemed busily engaged. "What problems, if any, do you face here, Bill?" I asked him.

I had the impression Bill didn't have any real concerns, but he did say, "My biggest issue is ensuring stock is rotated by date (earliest date out first), because retailers' purchases do vary. But there's not much I can do about that."

---

[1]   Large pieces of uncooked bacon, such as shoulders or gammon, are compressed in a machine and the meat forced out into a plastic 'stocking-like' shape – rather like the way sausages are produced, but on a bigger scale. The plastic used is a thick, inedible substance made from a strong viscose plastic. Each 'sausage' shape containing the bacon is clipped at each end by means of a metal clasp. This process allows the bacon to be more easily handled and cut on a slicing machine.

"Do you need any training for your people, Bill?"

"My supervisor trains any new staff, and I have little movement of processors. Once they know what they're doing, that's it," he informed me. My impression was that Bill was able to take a step back from the 'hands-on' work to deal with buying, assembling orders, and ensuring his bacon deliveries went out on time.

"Thanks, Bill. I'll let you get on with the good work," I said as I got ready to head off. Again, this department was on top of the job. No need for any training, but I did pick up the fact that whatever training was going on, it was not defined or written in a manual. Something I must do for all future training. No sign of anyone smoking; had they now been stopped from doing so, or had they seen me coming?

The afternoon was almost over, and I decided to head back to my office which had been made available for me on the first floor and fairly close to Harry. There, I found a handwritten note from Harry lying on my desk. "Please pop in to see me before you go this evening. Harry," it said. Some other 'mail' items had been left on my desk – nothing of any great importance: some trade magazines, including *The Grocer*, where I noticed my name had been added to the circulation list stapled to the front page. I was being gradually integrated to the life of the company.

I made a few telephone calls to fix times the next day to visit the Buying Manager and the Office Supervisor, and I began to plot some dates to visit the directors of the other divisions as per Harry's advice.

It was nearing 4.30pm and – after checking with Mary, Harry's secretary – I knocked on his office door.

"Aha! Still surrrrrviving then, are we?" came a booming voice. This was my boss's 'take off' of a Scottish accent, which was quite comical coming from a London East-Ender.

"Yes, I've been greeted happily," I assured him.

"Hope it lasts," he said with a wide grin. "So, what have you been up to?"

I gave a run down on my day. "Good," Harry remarked as he lit a tipped cigarette while we spoke. "The reason for us having a chat is that I'm planning a few improvements around the building. Not a massive budget, but I've got Board approval to do something – and you can help me."

I was amazed to hear this, for I'd given some passing thought about the building. Its offices and the external fabric were in a jaded, downbeat and neglected state. This was not a surprise, for my experience generally in the grocery trade had been that profit margins did not permit any big spending and I recalled the way that Wm Low had also acquired second-hand warehouse premises.

"What can I do to help?" I asked him.

"I'm going to upgrade the stonework and exterior painting of the office building on Blackness Road, and I want to increase the size and design of the windows on the ground floor to provide more light in the offices."

I nodded as he revealed his plans. "I did see that the street-level windows with the wire mesh coverings had obviously harboured dust, debris and grime over a long period of years, and the blistered flaky paintwork didn't help the image."

"The reason I want your help, Bob, is that I'm going to have the entire office area repainted... and I want your advice on the colour of paint!"

Here's a big one for you, Murray. Get it right, and Harry will be happy. Get it wrong, and the entire staff reaction could be damaging and accompanied by "That's the new training officer's fancy ideas." And would Harry accept any problems were his folly?

"Gee! Okay, Harry I'll think about that," I assured him.

"Don't take too long. The painters start next week, and they need to know what colour to buy. Here's the colour chart, by the way," he said, passing it to me over the top of his expansive desk.

"I'll let you know tomorrow," I declared with more certainty than I actually felt.

"There's something else, Bob," he told me. "I want to enhance the foyer floor area. What do you think: carpet, up-market lino, wood, or..." Harry paused for dramatic effect, then grinned, "...marble?"

"Good questions, Harry. I'll think about that too."

"You see, Bob, it's all part of staff morale – isn't it?"

"I agree," I replied earnestly.

"You'll know all about that from your management studies," Harry observed thoughtfully. "See you tomorrow."

And that was it – I'd never come across the subject of employee welfare as it related to the colour of internal paint or an entrance hall, but I sensed there could likely be a psychological theory behind it.

Come on now, Robbie Murray. Something to think about overnight. Simple enough tasks, but monumental mistakes if they go wrong.

When I arrived at the offices the next morning, it was to hear the news that one of our employees – while walking down Blackness Road the previous evening – spotted smoke billowing out of a bacon department window. The fire brigade had been called out and found some paper and cardboard material had started to smoulder, but luckily no flames were in evidence and nor was any serious damage done.

Making a mental note I looked forward to having a conversation sometime with Eddie about Bill's over-exuberant bacon smoking activities... or had the 'phantom smoker' left his cigarette end in a more (or less) dangerous place?

On a serious note, some discussion was going to be required.

CHAPTER 3

"Meeting Managers", or "Fighting the Big Supermarkets"

L ATER, while driving to Kirriemuir, I reflected on my day and Harry's request to provide advice on the colour of the office paintwork. It was clear that he wanted an immediate answer. My training officer remit was wider than I had imagined.

"Good morning, Harry. Is it okay to look in to speak?" I asked him over the phone on my desk.

"Of course!" came the reply.

I wasted no time in making my way from my office to his own. "Green paint!" I said as I closed the door behind me.

"Grrrrrreeeeeen!" exclaimed my boss with some relish.

"Yes... well, because of all the local 'fitba' talk I'd been picking up at lunchtimes, I had to eliminate partisan football colours. Blue of any shade, tan or orange, reds were all out. So I think a suitable 'non-football' green is the answer. I've also got a theory about colours which are comforting and calming, such as the 'green room' back-stage."

I recalled Harry telling me he had done some 'voice overs' for commercial products, and had been in a circle of friends which included Kenneth Williams, Sid James, Bernard Bresslaw and a few others. I hoped the green room reference may hit a favourable spot.

"Good Bob, leave me the chart and I'm sure we can agree something." He paused for a moment, then added hopefully: "And the entrance hall, Bob?"

"A good quality upmarket lino," I replied without hesitation.

"Why?"

"It'll be walked on a lot, and more easily cleaned."

"I'd really like good quality carpet, but my fellow directors think it would make us look like we're too rich. That would make it more difficult to plead poverty when looking for best discounts from suppliers. Upmarket lino may appear to give similar messages," he pondered aloud.

A thought occurred to me. "Why not carpet tiles then, Harry?" I suggested.

"Good thinking!" he agreed. "That's the answer. What colour?"

"Anything dark would do."

Ultimately, Harry picked out two novel modern shades of acceptable green paint – a darker shade up to dado height, and a lighter tint for walls above – with white ceilings. I'd no idea if the colours would have any favourable impact, but perhaps employees at least may eventually notice an attempt was being made to enhance their workplace.

* * *

My next visit was to meet Alex, the buying manager. Strategically, his office was on the first floor at the top of the stairs – a perfect spot where suppliers' sales representatives could wait. Alex had two assistants, and their work was determined and allocated on a products basis.

"Hello, Alex – pleased to meet you," I said by way of greeting.

"Hello, Bob," he replied with a smile. "Yes, the boss has told us of your arrival – I wish you all the best in your new post."

After some chat about the grocery trade and my previous experience with Wm Low & Co., I got to the point of asking Alex if he required any training for his team.

"I have always recruited buyers from within the retail grocery trade, so the knowledge they need comes with them," he told me. Alex explained that he looked after items which were deemed to have maximum 'promotions' impact for retailers – that is, cut-price products which would most likely appear on posters and window bills, and – more importantly – feature in newspaper advertising.

"We call them "KVI's," he explained.

"Yes, I'd heard of the term – 'Known Value Items'. But we didn't use the term in Willie Low's."

"It's important when we select cut-price items for promotion that we recognise that certain products which shoppers buy often can be promoted, as they will see a genuine bargain. It adds to the impression of being a real saving." Alex clarified that his assistants took care of purchasing other general grocery products, and linked with Douglas's Visapost system to gauge how much to buy.

"We have no marketing manager, Alex, so how do you get to the stage of creating a programme of promotions?" I asked him.

"Ah, good question. VG Central Office in London plans a programme of promotions twelve months in advance for the whole of the UK. That's thirteen separate four week-long promotions in a year. This means we can take up a full page in several Scottish daily newspapers, advertising the 'centrally organised' grocery items along with the items which I arrange separately. When I put an item in a promotion, I get a discount off the invoice or a long-term agreement (LTA) with the supplier. The more I buy, the bigger the discount. VG Central Office in London does its own negotiating."

"So, who finally decides which products go into a promotion?"

"So long as I follow VG's national promotions plan, I choose which products are added into the combined programme. We have to be careful we don't upset our suppliers: for example, if say, Velvet toilet rolls feature in a VG national promotion, I would have to include Andrex on separate dates – that keeps everyone happy."

"Can you explain that to me please, Alex?" I enquired, keen to know more about what was involved.

"Easy. Bowater Scott manufacture Andrex products, and a main competitor – Kimberley Clark – make Velvet products. So we must always avoid conflicting manufacturers' interests."

"What rules do you follow when designing a package of goods on promotion?"

"Excellent question, Bob. The fundamental point is that, as a wholesaler, we are trying to give the small retail grocer the best competitive edge possible."

"You mean to offer their customers goods at prices which can, as near as possible, match those of the 'big boys' such as Tesco and Sainsbury, and in Scotland we have to compete with Fine Fare, Massey and Willie Low."

Alex nodded in agreement. "Our objective is to bring low 'supermarket-like' prices to the small shop." He paused, then added: "We also have to beat competing voluntary group retailers."

"Who are the main competitors?" I asked.

"Mace, Vivo, A&O, and Centra... but the one to beat is Spar, if we can."

"How do you define a good promotion?"

"A VG promotion should attract housewives' attention. For example, promotions usually run for at least four weeks, and always contain canned products – that is, fruits, veg, meat, soups or jams, breakfast cereals... anything in fact that's popular on a household shopping list, keeping in mind KVI's."

"So, you have a large part to play in making profit for the division?" I prompted him.

"Well, it's a blend of my own promotions and VG national promotions, and of course my plans can be influenced by suppliers who come up with good deals."

"So those sales reps I see sitting outside your office have an impact too?"

"Yes, but we see fewer 'reps' these days. Suppliers are cutting down on costs of 'reps' on the road – they have negotiators at their head offices who speak directly with me on the phone."

"Yes, I remember in my Willie Low days that sales 'reps' lined up in the shop to speak to my boss and, in time, to me. Every manufacturer seemed to have a 'rep on the road', but that's fast disappearing." Thinking for a moment, I added, "I'd like to know what steps you take to communicate all your plans?"

"I have meetings with Harry and Alastair to keep them in the picture on expected discounts and bonuses, which are really extra profit. And of course I keep Alastair informed, so his consultants are aware. In addition to fascia boards and newspaper adverts, 'competitive prices' is the biggest benefit we can bring to retailers who pay a surcharge to be in the VG group."

"So when I see whole-page adverts for VG promotions, there will be identical advertisements in newspapers across the UK?" I wondered aloud.

"Yes, the nationally promoted items will be common for all wholesalers," he confirmed, "but each wholesaler will add their own negotiated products."

"I see. And do you link up with our Cash and Carry division in any way?" I asked.

"Good point. Yes, if I can link with Cash and Carry to do a promotion at the same time then the LTA income will be even greater for us all. Eddie here and Frank Keanie in Cash and Carry work together to maximise marketing income from suppliers."

Alex's phone then rang to say the rep from Bowater Scott had arrived on time for him, and our meeting closed. Although there was no marketing department within the division, it was a fascinating insight to know how much of an impact that department had on the sales and profit fortunes not only of the division, but of the company too.

* * *

One more department to visit – and I was still anxious to learn how invoices were sent to customers. I waited until after lunch and, as planned, went to meet Susan – the office manager.

I had learned initially that Eddie, the accountant – whilst described as Operations Manager – also had control over the office function and, as such, had direct access to check every element such as purchase and sales ledgers, and cash office.

I had my query ready. "One of my questions, Susan, is how are the retailers eventually charged for their purchases?"

"Come and I'll show you," she offered.

Susan guided me to the ground floor main office section, and we paused as she said "These ladies here are described as 'Listers'," indicating some nearby staff members.

"What does a Lister do?" I asked her.

"When the PLOF comes back upstairs from the warehouse, the girls here read every item picked and key in the amounts. They add on the appropriate VG service percentage charge, then staple the 'listing' on to the PLOF which is then taken to the warehouse despatch supervisor."

"So the 'picked' PLOF with the listing attached, plus the next new PLOF, all go out with the order and delivered by the driver?"

"Exactly," she confirmed. "Because of the huge mail load at Christmas, the PLOFS – to prevent being delayed in the post – are collected by the sales consultants. That way we can pick the order in good time."

In front of me were four young female office clerks keying in, at an amazing speed, every amount on what were basically adding machines with a paper printout. Thoughts returned of my worries in the early days of self-service when one checkout operator using what was basically an adding machine – then, just as now, all the profit depended on those high speed 'listers'.

Susan continued with a tour of the ledger offices and the cash office. My impression was of what a labour-intensive operation it was, and with so much paperwork. But the employee activity was impressive, and there was a vivid vibrancy emanating in every element of the division's operation.

"Any training needs here Susan?" I enquired once the tour was over.

"I have a fairly stable turnover of staff, but I always make sure I train 'spare' listers to fill unexpected absences," she told me.

Good news then, Robbie. Apart from the Sales and Warehouse departments, no immediate training required.

* * *

Looking back at that first week, I recalled how I had started to set up my office. The spartan small room with a partial view of the warehouse two storeys below me contained one desk, one chair and a filing cabinet. Still sitting in a folder – in the only file in the four-drawer cabinet – was the Distributive Industry Training Board's grant claim form.

The cost implication of this was that the Training Board had authority to charge each business in the distributive industry a 0.7% levy of the company annual wage bill, but there was a system whereby the company could obtain a discount for whatever recorded training was being carried out. Discounts varied: for example, if job descriptions existed for all job categories, ten percent of the total levy could be deducted. Similarly, if every new employee followed a designated induction training programme, a further ten percent could be waived. There was a list of identified key training 'milestones' which, if followed, would mean the company would escape the levy entirely. In my case I could expect only a five percent discount because, so far, the company had carried out a training needs assessment. The theory was that companies who trained would gain at the expense of those that didn't.

On examining the document, I had to conclude that W&P was unable to secure any further discounts. Therein lay the basis of a training programme.

There you are then, Robbie – your challenge lies ahead!

CHAPTER 4

"Space on a Ship", or "Branches or Depots"

IT was Monday afternoon and my second week of induction, and I looked forward to a more expansive view of the business activities by hearing from directors the scope of each division. The Chairman of the Board, Mr Herbert Philip, did not live near Dundee, but I had made arrangements for a brief meeting – as requested by Harry – with the other main Board directors, thanks to the help of their respective secretaries.

The order of meetings was determined purely by directors' availability, and it happened that I should meet Mr Frank Philip – Director of the Catering Division – that Monday afternoon. He occupied an office on the third floor which also accommodated the central corporate office, which handled the final accounting, financial and legal matters.

Of course, I fully realised that although I was the one seeking an insight into each divisions' operation, it was myself who was under scrutiny. Would Harry's judgement also be under the microscope?

"Come in, Mr Murray," Mr Philip said by way of greeting. "Pleased to meet you – how are you settling in?"

We shook hands. "Very well thanks, Mr Philip. I'm beginning to learn something about the VG operation."

"Yes, it's going very well – and Harry is intent on making it grow."

"I'm impressed by the hectic work rate all over that division."

Mr Philip was a most genial and courteous man, and came across as having a quiet leadership style. He told me he had been in the family business since his demob from the Army after the Second World War.

"What do you want, then? Mr Murray, or do I call you Bob?"

"Yes, I'm Bob – and although I'm working for Delivered Grocery, Harry thinks I should know what's going on across the company."

"Yes, well, that's good. But I can't afford you, Bob – and I probably need you more than Harry!" Frank Philip had a wonderful self-deprecating manner and an infectious smile. I immediately felt comfortable with this gentleman, but was wise enough to know that I dare not venture any over-familiarity.

"Last week I chatted with each department manager and picked up what happens in the VG world, so I'm pleased to hear about the Catering Division."

"Good for you, Bob. Well, catering is how W&P started – away back in 1873." Frank swivelled his chair around and picked up a small framed picture on a bookcase. "There you are – June 9th 1873: the original partnership signed by the founders, Thomas Watson and Joseph Philip."

"Ah, that's very interesting. How did they come to do that?" I asked him.

"Word has been passed down the generations, but the version I like best is that a ship with a cargo of flour docked at Ohio – bound for Dundee – was found to have spaces in the hold. With such an unsafe situation, the captain ordered a consignment of boxes of lard, the cheapest product available, to fill the gaps. On arriving in Dundee, two shipping clerks – Messrs Thomas Watson and Joseph Philip, both in their twenties – became aware of the excess lard, which had no destination. Faced with the excess supply of lard, they went around every chip shop, works' kitchens and bakers' premises in Dundee and the wider area, taking orders for inexpensive

"That's it, Joseph – we are now official partners in the Watson and Philip business. Let's see where this takes us!"

lard. In doing so they unwittingly created a customer base from nothing, began to import lard, and found a bigger market for other imported products relating to the catering trade."

"Young entrepreneurs," I reflected.

"Well, it seems so easy and obvious, but that was the start of W&P."

I felt slightly puzzled. "I haven't heard of a Mr Watson?"

"That's because the last Watson left the business around 1948," Mr Philip told me.

"I've read how many businesses were created by good fortune, and that is a really great story."

"It is, and here we are – a public company now, and flexing our muscles to grow."

"So, Dundee was obviously the first depot and others followed," I observed.

"Yes, they started with a small warehouse in a narrow lane in the city centre then moved to Craig Street near the docks, but in 1898 the enterprising young chaps opened a branch in Aberdeen – then a very busy and important fishing port."

"Where are the depots located now, Mr Philip?"

"I don't mean to correct you, but in catering we use the word 'branch'. Cash and Carry division use the word 'depot'," he told me.

"Oh, sorry."

"There's a reason. I'll tell you about in a moment." He paused. "Today there are catering branches in Aberdeen, Newhaven (Edinburgh), Glasgow, and of course here."

"I see all fairly recently added?"

"Yes, I've developed the business since the war. Adapting old warehouses."

"Why the word 'branch', Mr Philip?" I enquired.

"I believe you have studied management, Bob. Well, I have a hands-off method (you probably have a technical word for it). You see, I leave my branch managers with total discretion to run their business."

At first, I was quite stunned by Mr Philip's statement, but I quickly realised there would be good reason. My quizzical look must have registered. "Don't get me wrong, Bob. I visit the branches regularly and hear what's going on in the trade – what's going up and what's going down. My managers know best what their customers' needs are, and Glasgow, Edinburgh and Aberdeen's needs differ from those of Dundee."

"Yes. I can follow that," I said.

"I never have my managers together for meetings. They jealously guard their own trading ideas. I attempted it a long time ago, and they simply tried to show off against each other and wanted to be seen as the best. It was a waste of everyone's time, including mine. So, I visit them, chat, take them for an evening meal and listen, and I'm the cross-fertiliser of ideas without them knowing the source. I simply pass on what appear to be my ideas, and encourage them to believe it's their own ideas. You see, it gives them huge independence. In fact, their customers probably don't know about me. For example, Mr Green – the branch manager at Aberdeen – is, to all intents, Mr Watson and Philip as far as his customers are concerned."

"I know delivered grocery have a budgetary control process – do you have the same?"

"Yes, all I want to achieve is an agreed profit growth figure every year. I leave my managers to deal with control of costs and stock levels," he explained.

"I can see the merits of all that, Mr Philip. Do you ever have any disappointments?" I asked him.

"Not so far, Robert," said the charming gentleman, with a genuine and trusting smile.

Mr Philip was a true father of the business and had a successful working methodology, and I was left to guess that each year's budget setting may be quite nervous for the Board – but obviously, so far, his approach worked. Hearing how the division operated was so engrossing, my time with Mr Philip passed very quickly. I had run well over the planned time he was to make available to me.

"Thanks for giving me your time, Mr Philip, and providing all that background – it's very helpful," I assured him.

"I wish you well with Harry. And if there's anything more you want to know about catering, let me know."

As I walked back to my office, I had a strong feeling I had joined a company with a real 'heart'. It underlined my decision to join, as Harry had said, 'a progressive company looking to grow'.

Robbie, don't be fooled by the gentle style of Mr Frank – he will have a clever depth knowledge of his trade. He's a genuine man and obviously much respected.

* * *

After such an absorbing afternoon with Mr Frank Philip, I was looking forward the following day to chat with the Cash and Carry Director, Mr J.B. Thomson. His office was in a separate area accessed via the vehicle workshop and Larch Street, a back street behind the VG warehouse.

Having avoided partisan paint colours for Harry's re-decorating plan, I was secretly amused when I saw tangerine painted walls and black skirting boards (the Dundee United FC colours) on the external walls of Mr Thomson's office. "Come in!" was the loud voice in response to my knock. "Ah, it's Bob Murray!" he smiled, accompany his greeting with an energetic handshake.

I was tempted to comment, as a joke, that I liked his paint colours and ask if he supported Dundee FC (dark blue), but one never knows how insulted a football fan may be. Mr Thomson seemed a down-to-earth, straight-talking, practical man, and amazingly – having heard Harry say one of his London friends was Sid James – here in front of me was a 'Sid James lookalike'.

"Hello, Mr Thomson. Thanks for seeing me," I said.

"Sit ye down. Coffee?" he offered.

"Tea, if that's possible, please, Mr Thomson."

"It's Jim," he assured me as he slid a hatch open to where his secretary was sitting next door. "Margaret, my usual – and a tea for Mr Murray, please."

"Thanks. I'm Bob," I told him.

"Yes, I know. You were teaching in the college a few years ago, weren't you?"

"That's right," I nodded, "but I'm back in the real world again."

Being thought of as a teacher in a deeply practical wholesale grocery environment was, I felt, not a good link, and I was quick to play it down.

"You were also a Willie Low manager, I believe?"

"Yes, that's right. I managed three branches over a three-year period," I told him.

"Then you left," he observed.

45

For the first time I felt that leaving Low's seemed like a disadvantage – as though I'd left the practical world behind me. I had to think carefully how to respond. "A lot of change was going on, and looking back I think I was put off by the worries of self-service and losing control of profit."

"What do you mean, Bob?" queried Jim.

Suddenly I felt a need to be clear "There was the move to checkouts , or glorified adding machines as I described them, with no checks and controls. It was impossible to feel safe. No till roll, and no way of knowing if money was being lost."

"I see," he said. "I'd never thought about that angle."

"Being only 23 years old back then, I found older managers – with the same worries – gave me a lot of bad, negative views about the direction of things."

"I see your point," he said, before changing the subject: "What do you want to know about Cash and Carry then, Bob?"

"A general run-down on depots and customers is fine," I replied.

"Right, you probably know that W&P became a public company only two years ago, when cash and carry, delivered grocery, catering and import were split into separate operating divisions – each with its own management and accounts. Before all that, my main job was to develop VG and get that side of the company established. I was then given the job of developing Cash and Carry."

"I'd be grateful if you would give me a general picture of what a cash and carry does, please," I asked him.

"Sure. We're basically a supermarket for small retail grocers, but our customer profile base is wider than that – we serve pubs, social clubs, cafes, restaurants and staff canteens. Our depots have around 2,000 to 4,000 registered customers.

"What kind of problems do you encounter?"

"Ah, the problems are varied – we have big problems with pilfering, so we sometimes share Harry's security officer. But we have to balance strict controls with customer loyalty. We also have problems trying to gauge off-take of seasonal goods; we can never be sure how our customer demands will go."

This was all interesting information. "How are your promotions arranged, Jim?" I asked him.

"We try to give money-off incentives by seeking better discounts from suppliers reps."

"What's the competition like?"

"Good question. There's a lot out there: Alliance, Martex (C.J. Lang, Dundee), Belvue, McNabs, Lonsdale, Stokes, Makro... to name a few. It's a tough market place, Bob."

"How many depots do you operate, Jim?" I enquired.

"Currently five: Dundee, Kilmarnock, Paisley, Greenock and Kirkcaldy, and looking to develop more."

"I'd like to look around Dundee sometime, if that's possible," I suggested to him.

"Let's have our 'cuppie', and then I'll show around."

"Yes, please. That would be great."

"This depot was previously a linen mill," he explained. "As a rule, we don't build; we adapt existing buildings. Linen mills are ideal for cash and carry – they're on one level, and an ideal size: up to around five or more thousand square feet."

Here was another example of utilising an old building. "You won't need a high building, I presume?" I remarked.

"Correct; I need space for customers to walk about wide aisles with trolleys, and an undercover area where they can load up their cars."

Jim's secretary brought the drinks and we continued chatting. "What's the most important aspect about running cash and carries?" I asked him, genuinely intrigued.

"Without doubt, marketing," he told me.

"How does that work?"

"My customers, in the main, are the small, family-run corner shops – not quite as organised as the VG members who pay a service charge, but nevertheless they want to promote an image of cost savings for the customer. Especially booze and fags, and a few other eye-catchers. When we go downstairs to the depot, I'll show you our marketing approach."

"Do you do promotions like VG?" I asked him.

"Yes, Frank my marketing manager next door looks after that."

"Do you advertise in the press?"

"No, when we run promotions, we hand out posters and handbills at the depot or distribute around the shops. Keep in mind our customers work in cash, so they are flexible." At that point Jim tapped his nose with his index finger. "Come, let's go."

As we left his office, Jim knocked loudly on the door next to his. He opened it and announced, "This is Bob Murray. I'm taking him downstairs to see the depot."

Frank, a smart-looking young man about my age, was speaking on the phone with his feet up on the desk in front of him. He gave me a wave and a wide, grinning smile while animatedly having a hearty conversation with someone on the other end of the line.

Once at street level, Jim pointed out the covered loading area used by his customers and took me to see a cramped-looking goods-in area. He guided me through the aisles, pointing out various departments and a secure area where cigarettes were stored and distributed. On the way, I was introduced to the manager, George McDonald – a smartly-dressed, efficient-looking man – every inch a grocer. "Hi Bob," he said in a friendly tone. "It's good to meet you. All the best – and remember, you can look in any time on our Friday late evening shopping time. But all wholesale packs – no single jars and cans. And cash only!" George laughingly made his point.

Jim and I walked on. "Here's our current handbill," he told me as he picked up an A4 printed mini-poster at the checkout. "And here's a blank trader's card that we issue to registered traders."

"Is it all strictly cash, Jim?" I queried.

"Absolutely! We have enough problems without chasing debts like George McLaren, Harry's security officer, has to do."

"So do you have security problems, Jim?"

"Aye, and I'm seriously thinking of employing a full-time security officer," he told me.

"What are the issues?" I asked him.

"Pilfering. You've no idea how many tricks retailers get up to by concealing fags and booze, so I need their boxes examined at the checkout."

As I looked around, I again saw that same level of activity I'd seen in Delivered Grocery; there was that air of busy industry. It was the tempo of grocery life I had experienced in my Willie Low days.

"I'm heading back up to my office now, Bob. I wish you well. Keep in touch if you need any more info," he offered.

"Thanks for the background and tour – and the tea!" I said gratefully in response. Jim Thomson, I could tell, was a real driving force, and it was easy to see how his charismatic and dynamic attitude had so successfully developed VG across Scotland. He was now using these same qualities to develop cash and carry.

After having another look around the depot and a chat with George McDonald, I returned to my office when I marvelled at two aspects – the time and consideration directors afforded me, a new arrival, and for the genuine warmth of the welcome.

Robbie, another impressive director – a different style from Mr Frank, but J.B. has a dynamic approach. He's very much 'a mover and a shaker'. Value the time they are giving you.

CHAPTER 5

"Strong Characters", or "The Chairman Says 'Hello'"

BEFORE the week was over, I had to fit in meetings with Mr Iain Philip, the Import Director, and with Mr Hadden, the Finance Director. Luckily, I had a phone call from Veronica – secretary for Mr Philip – asking if I could bring my meeting forward, as he had to fly 'down south' to England. He could see me for a few minutes before he departed.

We met on Thursday. Although I knew vaguely what to expect with the other operating divisions, the prospect of learning something about importing held some mystique.

"Come in!" was the bellow from inside his office when I knocked on Mr Philip's door. He occupied a spacious room, and his secretary was based in his office. Mr Philip was a tall, heavily-built man with a ruddy complexion. I had recognised him on a few occasions while he parked his Triumph Stag. When he stood up to shake my hand, I was surprised to see he was wearing a kilt.

"Sorry, Mr Murray," he assured me. "I don't want to be rude, but I thought it best to say my hello before setting off."

"Very good of you to fit me in. I really just wanted to say 'hello' because Mr Gardner asked me to introduce myself to the directors."

"I'm out of the office a lot," Mr Philip explained. "I travel all over the place. I'm off to Greece tomorrow at an early hour; next year's harvest price negotiations, you know."

Realising the unusual situation, I quickly realised there was little point in going in to detail. "I think Harry merely wanted me to show face, that's all."

"Good God, sir – if you can train me to get better deals in Greece, or anywhere else for that matter, let me know," he boomed.

I felt an urge to say something about Greece being a more comfortable place than suffering a Scottish January, but I didn't know him well enough. "I have no experience of the import world – is it currants that you buy in Greece?" My grocery product studies with The Grocers' Institute came to mind.

"My dear boy," he said, clearing his throat, "I buy everything from Canadian flour, Italian cherries, Australian raisins to Nigerian cacao and God knows what else!" He didn't reply to my 'currants' question – perhaps I had struck the wrong chord with my enquiry.

This was a new world for me, and all I could think of saying was something along the lines of, "So, do you import and then sell on in this country?"

"I import then sell to bakers, confectioners, Uncle Tom Cobley... and of course for use in our factory," he told me.

"Factory?" I asked, surprised. "I didn't realise the company had a factory."

"Ah yes, sir. You see, one learns something new every day in W&P! Yes, we process raw materials into products for the bakery trade such as chocolate vermicelli, mixed peel and so on."

This was valuable knowledge. "Where is the factory located, Mr Philip?"

"Near Glasgow. Kirkintilloch, actually."

"It's not part of my remit, but it would be interesting to visit someday."

"You'd be welcome... but Harry won't want you wasting time with me," he said.

"True." I had the feeling Iain Philip would not entertain the need for training. He was already grabbing his overcoat from the stand.

"Well, Mr Murray, I must dash. I have to drive four hours to bloody Abbotsinch Airfield (Glasgow Airport) for my flight. I wish you good luck in W&P."

"Thanks – and safe travelling." In an instant he was gone, leaving Veronica with a last complimentary comment.

"He's always so busy - rushing everywhere." Veronica remarked in a diplomatic tone.

Mr Iain is a very confident individual, and I'm sure knows his import business inside out. I surmised he would be a force to be reckoned with in his price negotiating. Unlikely you will be doing any training in the Import Division. Relax, Robbie.

* * *

A picture of the diverse and dynamic world of Watson and Philip was emerging, and my next meeting during my introductory period was arranged through Rachel to meet Mr Hadden in his office – just along the corridor from Mr Iain Philip. During my interview with Harry, I'd been introduced to Mr Hadden. Hearing a reply to my knock, I stepped inside.

"Hello?"

"Hello, Mr Hadden." Upon my arrival, he promptly motioned me to sit in a chair opposite him at his desk. Despite no handshake or any other welcome words, he was friendly and smiling, and looked as much a bank manager or headmaster as he did an accountant.

"Well, first impressions?" he prompted me.

"Excellent," I replied, "and I feel comfortable. It's a busy place, and very welcoming."

"Good. You'll find people co-operate well. What are your plans, then?"

This was the most searching question I'd had from any director. "First, I've got to respond to the DITB levy and claim form."

"I've seen the form. Just get someone here to help you check the figures."

"That's great. I was going to ask about double checking the wage bill figure," I observed.

"The figure should be basic pay and salaries. We don't need to include bonuses." This was good accounting advice from Mr Hadden, obviously an experienced professional.

"Thanks. I'll check with Head Office before I complete the form."

"Whoa, whoa!" he cried. "Hold on a minute. We don't have a head office here."

"I'm sorry, I thought head office came under your control," I responded, a little confused.

"I head up a *Central Office*. We don't have a Head Office in Watson and Philip." My immediate thought was that Mr Hadden was being pedantic about the title, but then he went on to explain. "My strong belief is that Head Offices have a tendency to tell people what to do, or 'talk down' to operating people. Watson and Philip's Central Office is here to support the operating divisions and provide our customers (the divisions) with a service. We are the servants, not the controllers."

"Ah, I see the point. Sorry, nobody so far had explained that to me. Yes, of course – I understand the thinking." My immediate thought was that perhaps the DITB form ought to be signed off by Mr Hadden himself since it would be an audited pay figure available only from his office, but of course DITB also wanted training information collected – hence my involvement. However, I felt the form's completion to be my responsibility.

"What training plans have you in mind, Bob?" Mr Hadden asked me, leaning back in his chair.

"Too early for details, but the warehouse manager wants order pickers and forklift truck drivers trained, and Alastair wants his VG Consultants trained. Of course, he also is concerned to have his consultants and retailers trained for decimalisation."

"Just be sure you don't dash in too quickly," he counselled.

"Yes, it's early days. I'll set my own pace."

It was excellent advice from Mr Hadden, with whom I instantly felt a rapport. Although in different situations we both had to offer our professional service to the divisions.

"Just don't rush in too quickly, otherwise you'll over-whelm yourself."

"Thanks for the advice, Mr Hadden," I responded.

"Okay, good luck. Take a measured approach." And then, as an afterthought: "When will your family be joining you?"

"Hopefully in the spring, if I have house ready by then. There's a new arrival expected in summer, so I must be organ-ised by then."

On my way back to my office, I marvelled at Mr Had-den's 'service to divisions' approach, his helpful advice, and his friendly concern about my personal circumstances. It was con-firmation that there existed in the business what appeared to be a healthy balance between the Central Office's professional expertise, the trading instincts within the divisions and the added interest with people.

* * *

As I approached my office, I met Harry's secretary Mary in the corridor. "Harry hopes to see you before the end of the day," she told me.

Taking a few minutes to check my desk for messages, I went to see my boss. The light indicating 'enter' was lit up, so – knocking on his door first – I looked in to meet him.

"Ah, the very man!" he exclaimed in greeting. "How's it going?"

"Where do I start, Harry?" I chuckled, amazed at the amount of information I had gained in just a few short hours.

"The beginning would do!"

"I've learned we have a factory and no head office."

Harry grinned widely as he lit a cigarette and placed it in his cigarette holder. "Good, isn't it?" He seemed to enjoy my discoveries. "Jim (by which he meant Mr Hadden) is very strong about a Central Office."

"I fully understand his viewpoint."

"He looks after every penny – even his middle name reflects that." Harry's humour spilled out: "Yes, he's James Coyne Hadden! And Mr Iain, did he burst your ear drums?" Harry beamed.

"He seems an energetic man and a colourful character," I responded diplomatically.

"He's certainly a *lively* character – travels the world in his kilt, being the trrrrrrusty Scottish businessman!"

"An interesting facet in the business."

"Aye, but his profit contribution is now a bit more transparent since we went public with separate divisions. Tell me about my department managers – that's more important to me."

"There's no doubt there is an excellent work ethic, Harry. Each manager is very much hands-on, with a real grip of the basics. Douglas wants forklift drivers and pickers trained. His problem is damages on badly-packed cages. Alastair is looking to train his consultants on developing business, and also wants retailers and his consultants ready for decimalisation."

"Sounds sensible. Just get on with it, Bob," he declared with confidence.

"Most of this was flagged up when I did the training needs analysis," I observed.

"I remember."

"This is a new experience for me, but I can see it's a 'tight ship' with no fat. I'm impressed by the hard work of the smaller department heads – buying, bacon and printing, all with a small workforce. I don't see big improvements being possible in productivity. The office is quite diverse I think there could be gains in moving staff around to fill in gaps as and when they occur. Labour turnover is greatest in warehouse, transport and office, so induction training would be helpful there."

Harry stroked his chin, seeming thoughtful. "So what's your plan, Bob?"

"A plan *is* necessary, and I'll draw up some details and dates," I assured him.

"Good," he said, adding: "and what did you learn about the other divisions?"

"Mr Herbert Philip is the only director I haven't met, but I was kindly received by everyone – they gave me good background to the company. Especially Mr Frank Philip."

"Have you worked them all out yet?"

"Well, as brothers they have a practical approach to their own work – they are certainly not directors merely by name."

"They each have specialities," he explained, "but they are not all brothers."

I was surprised. "Aren't they?"

"No. Herbert and Frank are, but Iain is a cousin."

"I like Frank's delegated responsibility," I told him.

"Aye, it seems to work... but a bit risky if and when a branch manager leaves us or dies."

"Yes, I wondered if he would have a succession plan."

"To be honest, probably not," Harry said.

"I've seen the delivered grocery warehouse and Jim Thomson showed me around Cash and Carry, but although I had an interesting chat with Mr Frank about catering I haven't yet seen a catering branch."

"Why don't you ask Frank if you can pop into see young Peter? That's Herbert's son. He's manager of the Dundee branch."

Another useful suggestion. "Thanks, Harry. I will."

"What do you think of Mr Hadden's Central Office philosophy?" he asked me.

"It's commendable. Does it work?"

"Aye," (again Harry's Scottish accent take-off) "it seems to. I like his approach. He worked for an American company here in Dundee, and introduced a clever budgeting control system. Mr Herbert is thrilled with it because, for the first time the company – being public – requires it, but it's also a great tool for controlling costs all over the company. You'll see how it works soon!"

I'd never, previously, had an opportunity to study directors and managers in any business, and I felt privileged that my boss was so frank and trusting of me to discuss such confidential views. It signalled to me that, in turn, I could raise any confidential matter with him.

"What else did you discover?" he prompted me.

"Because it would have appeared out of place, I resisted asking any questions about the profit contribution from each division. What is the profit earning breakdown?"

"Ah! That's a good point – let me try to sum that up. You'll know from your retail world about gross and net profits- so let me give you some broad ideas: Catering runs at around 20% to 25% gross and a net of around 6% to 10%. Cash and Carry will be closer to retail figures somewhere around 10 to 15% with a net of 4 or 5 %. And here's the tricky one – Delivered Grocery 'scrapes up' about 6 or 7% gross, if we're lucky. And – wait for it – between 0.5% and 1.5%.net. Import is smaller scale, but profit percentage is somewhere between catering and Cash and Carry... though variable. Now you see how much volume we need to put through my ware-house to make some decent money, AND that's why you see a tight ship. If it wasn't, we wouldn't survive."

"That's quite a range of profit earning ability," I said.

"And that's the beauty of this group – we have that ability to come out with a decent average profit, and that sta-bility is important – especially as we are a public company with investors."

"Yes, I can see why that's important." But I had anoth-er question. "What is the total number of employees in each division?"

"It's around 450 in the Group. As you know, the figure is approaching 200 in Delivered Grocery, and there's over a hundred in each of Catering and Cash and Carry. The balance is made up of Central Office and Import. But you haven't mentioned Cash and Carry yet. How did you get on with J.B.?"

"J.B.?" I asked, perplexed.

"Yes, to distinguish him from Eddie."

"I see. Yes, he was brilliant too – he showed me around the depot, and told me all about the need for strong market-ing."

"Jim has a fantastic history in W&P. The story is that when he was the manager in charge of deliveries to retail gro-cers, he warned the Board in 1959 that Cash and Carry was developing rapidly in England and would soon come to Scot-land. He convinced the board to immediately beat their city rivals C.J. Lang and open the first Cash and Carry in Dundee. Later in the sixties, when the London-based VG Group was seeking to award franchises across the UK, it was Jim who won the VG franchise for Scotland. Then, single-handedly, he got VG off the ground in Scotland. He was really the pioneer for this division, and now he's developing Cash and Carry."

Clearly he was quite the innovator. "I could see his down to earth, no-nonsense approach," I told Harry.

"That's how businesses grow, and that's why the divisions are headed up by pioneers."

It was the end of my first inside look into how the group was run, and it provided me with a huge and comforting understanding of the latent strengths that lay within the business. Can you imagine joining a company and finding the opposite?

My induction was over, and it so happened that one of the last meetings was a casual one with Eddie. One day after the dissection around the table about of Scotland's chances in the World Cup in the summer, we found ourselves the last two at the lunch table. We chatted, and he asked me how I'd got on. I gave him a general run-down on my experiences, and while doing so found myself very carefully not giving away any of the confidences from directors or from Harry. Eddie was trying to get the 'lie of the land'.

"By the way, Eddie, I was impressed by Bill's bacon department," I mentioned.

"Were you really? Well, I'll bet you half a crown you'll never find another cigarette end in the smoked streaky bacon."

"You're on, Eddie!"

It was later that same evening I heard on the TV news that, in preparation for decimalisation, half-crowns had just been removed from circulation. Eddie had that kind of humour, but I also found him a serious-minded and clever man.

A week or so later on, a board meeting day, a large gentleman with great 'presence' came into my office and seemed immediately to fill it. "How are you getting on Mr Murray?" he asked me.

"Very well, thanks." My stunned expression must have been obvious to him.

"Herbert Philip, Chairman," he introduced himself, extending his hand.

I must confess to being somewhat awestruck. "Pleased to meet you, Mr Philip."

"Harry tells me you're getting nicely involved."

"Yes, I'm beginning to know people," I assured him.

"Just dashing to a meeting," he said. "Good – keep up the good work." And with a broad smile, he was gone.

My worry was that I had not actually done any 'good work' yet.

Well, Robbie Murray. That's your intro to W&P almost over. Next stage is the 'doing' bit, to justify your appointment. You've probably had a closer look than most new starters into the hearts and minds of the people who run the company. Can't ask any more than that! And even the Chairman is prepared to give you some time, too!

CHAPTER 6

January 1970 to August 1970
"Sale by Public Roup", or
"Flags"

AS I walked out of a lawyer's city centre office I felt a tug on my coat sleeve. "Are you interested in buying this property, sir?" came the pointed question.

"Yes, I am," I replied.

"Would you like to come to my office to discuss the matter?"

"No, sorry I can't do that – my lawyer instructed me that if I attended this meeting, I should be 'bound and gagged'."

"Oh, I see," he said. "Can you give me your name, please?"

"No, sorry, but I will report to my lawyer and he may call you," I told him.

"That's good," was the only response.

This procedure alarmed me slightly, as I had seen the property in Wormit – a village at the south end of the Tay Rail Bridge – and although it needed some work, I felt it was a good prospect and any delay may result in losing the chance to buy.

As requested, I phoned my solicitor and reported on the meeting. "How did the public roup go then, Mr Murray?" asked Mr Wanless.

"I arrived before 11 o'clock and found a large room full of men, possibly about twenty," I told him. "Exactly at eleven o'clock, one of three men sitting at the top table read the details of the three-bedroom property with details of feu duty and price. He then asked the assembled group in the room that any offers for the property be made. He gave three opportunities for offers to buy, each time resulting in silence."

"Yes, that sounds like a typical public roup. Are you still interested in the property?"

"Yes, I am."

"Would you like me to convey your offer of the asking price of £4,600, subject to survey?" he enquired.

"Please do," I responded.

Later, my solicitor phoned to say he had left a verbal offer of £4,600. I asked my representative why, with the room full of people, no offers had been made, and he explained the house was being sold as a result of bankruptcy and the men would have been legal representatives of the lenders looking for some 'shillings in the pound".

The next day, my lawyer called me to say "a woman in Glasgow" was also interested in the property and was to make an offer. I had, over prior years, purchased three properties and was alert to my suspicion of 'lawyers upping tactics'. Calculating that, if it was true, I guessed "the woman" may possibly offer £5,000 and – if the invisible lady may go even higher, say to £5300 – I decided to make a tactical offer of £5,301.

Whatever happened, my supposition and tactic – if it was genuinely required – succeeded, and I secured the purchase. I could now push on to sell my place in St Ives. It was late January, and I had good time to make the property ready for occupation.

By good fortune, the property in England sold with an entry day in April, and we were able to live in Kirriemuir until I had made ready the house in Wormit. During February and March I developed a routine of leaving the office early each evening at 5.30 pm, had a sandwich in a pub in Newport, and systematically painted the rooms and tidied up the Wormit home so that my furniture van was able to collect all our household effects from the St Ives property before the owners moved in.

On a cold, wet July evening with a swirling thick hill mist on the road from Kirriemuir, I negotiated the winding route in time to see Carys' baby sister, the new arrival Wendy, make her appearance in Dundee Royal Infirmary at 1.45 am on 8th July. There were no visitors except for husbands in those days, but the next day – while in the hospital car park – I was able to hold Carys up in my arms while she waved up to her baby sister held by her mother at a ward window. Two weeks later, after ten months of separation, the whole family were together under one roof in Wormit.

* * *

Meanwhile, life at W&P had to go on, and I discovered supervising moving our belongings out of the house in St Ives coincided with the division's annual staff dinner dance at the

Invercarse Hotel, Dundee. Thus although I had organised the event, it meant I could not attend.

The first hiccup in my new job came after another function during that April. In those early unfair, divisive days, the drivers and warehouse employees in delivered grocery division were not invited to the annual office dinner dance. A separate function was organised for them. My brief was to find a venue where they could get drinks and a meal and, ideally, facilities such as darts, dominoes and cards.

It became obvious by facts I was given that, historically, several venues had previously been used and, in my ignorance, I had no contacts or knowledge of a suitable untried venue in Dundee until I found a wayside pub in Fife which seemed to offer all my needs. I had visited the venue, spoken with the owner, arranged prices and organised a bus to and from the pub.

On my return from England, I was met with disturbing reports that the drivers' and warehouse event had turned nasty with bad behaviour, drunkenness and damage to property. Most regrettably, the pub was a customer of the Catering Division, which added to my growing alarm and disappointment.

No criticism came my way, but it was an unfortunate start and a wake-up call to me about the future handling of such events. Looking back, had the 'divisive' policy created that rowdy incident in Fife? Following the embarrassing behaviour, the principle of organising separate functions was debated at management meetings. It seems amazing today that weekly paid employees had been treated in such an unacceptable way.

You can't win them all, Murray. Sometimes in life a bad event will actually bring good. But it's something to think about for the future.

* * *

In earlier years I had never had the opportunities, nor the colleagues, to take a great interest in FIFA World Cup tournaments, but with lunchtime gatherings I had my first experience of hearing the chat. In 1970 it was Bobby Brown who managed the Scotland squad, and the hope was that we may manage to qualify – but with Austria, West Germany and Cyprus in the group it was an ambitious call. Well-informed colleagues who knew a lot about football were edging towards Scotland qualifying. We beat Austria and Cyprus and required a win to get to round one. To the dismay around our table, we lost 3-2 against West Germany. Alas! But it provided weeks of analysis and friendly teasing.

After my April trip to England, I was invited to join Alastair at each of the upcoming six VG retailers' local meetings in order to deal with questions that may arise about the forthcoming switch to decimalisation in February 1971. I was told that questions invariably arose relating to delivery or warehouse problems, and sometimes PLOF and listing issues. As a result Eddie would also attend all meetings.

The six locations were visited over a two-week period, commencing with the 'home' base meeting in Invercarse Hotel. Thereafter, meetings were held at the Langstracht Hotel in Aberdeen, the McDonald Hotel in Glenrothes, the Coatbridge Hotel, the Seamills Hotel in West Kilbride and the Tontine Hotel in Greenock. Alastair's routine was to leave early each day in order to hold afternoon meetings with consultants and retailers. Consequently I found myself driving Eddie to each location in time for the meeting, and gaining valuable time to learn more about each other while discussing confidential business-related matters.

In those days it took nearly two hours to drive to Aberdeen via the coastal towns route. To reach Glenrothes and Coatbridge, two hours driving to each was also required, and the West Kilbride and Greenock trips each took almost four hours. This was prior to dual carriageways and flyovers across Glasgow, resulting in painfully slow driving on country roads and through Glasgow city streets.

Alastair always had retailing matters to introduce or address, and I found the meetings an excellent customer relations exercise while the exposure of problems provided myself and Eddie with an insight into training needs or organisational and procedural problems and solutions which I enjoyed discussing with him.

The work to set up the meeting room, layout chairs and deal with visual aids all helped to develop a valuable team spirit, especially since it seemed my new colleagues were all of similar age and level within the division's structure. Becoming an active participant – setting the 'stage', dimming lights and advising on visual aids – I was in my element and, I hope, helped provide a professional atmosphere.

At each meeting Alastair introduced me and, although it was 'early days', I gave a short run-down on how I hoped we could help with the change to decimals. I reassured them that we would organise 'hands-on' training when it became clear what visual aids would exist. I also added that it was likely new decimal coins would be available and we would do some practical cash handling exercises. Retailer meetings offered a valuable opportunity to develop working relationships and helped to create trust within the team.

Good opportunity to help with your teaching and training skills, Murray!

* * *

At divisional management meetings chaired by Harry, every aspect with a bearing on efficiency and profitability was discussed and each department head gave a report. Training activity was reported by myself.

In answer to Harry's 'around the table' question about employees' reactions to the exterior building improvements and repainting of the offices, there were favourable responses from managers. Encouraged by this, Harry suggested that he wanted to consider making use of the three flagpoles which had evidently been fixed for many years to the building facing Blackness Road. My reading of his idea was that he wanted to enhance the entire appearance of the newly spruced-up premises.

After discussion about which flags, when to fly and how to deal with them, I sensed that managers – each with strict disciplines about costs, sales and profits – seemed a little lukewarm about spending time and money on the matter. I wasn't wrong, and it was left to me to come up with some proposals. In the meantime, Harry arranged to have joiner John scrape off the blistered paint, repaint poles white and fit new cords.

It was also left with me to initially speak with security man George, a retired Dundee city police officer (and a keen Tay swimmer and New Year 'dooker') to ascertain the protocol for flying flags, as I had in mind through my Boy Scout days that there were strict rules. After discussing with George, it was indeed the case that Watson & Philip would be required to lower flags overnight, ensure the Union Jack flew higher than any other flags, and we could fly only the Union Flag and the Scottish Saltire but no other Royal Scottish flag.

After further discussion, it was decided to buy a Union Flag and a Saltire, making sure the former was the larger. The idea of flying a 'W&P flag' on third flagpole was added to the agenda for later discussion. It was questioned that in order to comply with dropping flags at night, how would someone gain access to the flagpoles? It was discovered that the only route was via an open window from Harry's office followed by a walk along the duckboards on the warehouse roof – or provide joiner John with a long ladder to do the necessary each evening at close of business. To test the practicality, I found myself, George and John climbing through Harry's office window and walking along the part-glass roof of the warehouse, with a potential fifty-foot fall through a suspect roof if we accidentally put a foot wrong.

A final decision was made: we would fly a large Union Flag in the centre, and smaller Saltires at each side until a company flag could be commissioned. It was also decided, because of the dangers and the questionable use of John Devine's time, not to lower the flags each evening.

Following the trials and tribulations of Harry's simple idea, the subject of flags became a humorous discussion point and a by-product was the 'fun and games' discussion which absorbed so much valuable time, yet produced a bonding amongst the management team. Flags were not likely to earn any extra profit.

After a few weeks of loyally flying our magnificent flags, disaster struck when George. without knocking on Harry's door, interrupted a management meeting while we were discussing the several options for a company flag to declare, in the manner of a policeman's proclamation, "the problem of the flags has been concluded."

We all looked up at George in dumb amazement and then he added, "They've been stolen!"

George's face was a strange picture of glee and dismay. A twinkling eye reflected his humour, after all the serious discussion, of the sheer irony that one of his duties was to prevent theft! Harry almost choked as he spluttered out a mouthful of coffee, and everyone gasped.

Two mysteries remained: why had none of us noticed their absence that morning, and who stole the flags? Did they end up at a Scottish football or rugby game, or had the 'flag police' decided we had broken the 'lowering' rule?

There was a weary guffaw around the table, and then Harry said – with some noticeable relief and a broad smile – "Okay, take 'company flag' off the agenda!"

* * *

As the year rolled on, the subject of decimalisation took on a greater significance. The earlier focus had been on retailers' training, but it became obvious that a far greater impact would be felt within the company with everything from invoicing, record keeping paperwork, repricing, banking and printing PLOFS all requiring attention. The extent of the effect was recognised and a committee, to meet on a two-weekly basis, was set up and chaired by Mr Hadden. It became normal practice to have a 'post-meeting' gathering –

once again it was an opportunity for 'gelling' with team-mates. Eddie instituted a lunch at his home which we regularly enjoyed. I recall my first visit to his home.

"What's the significance of the colours on your garage door, Eddie?" I asked him out of genuine curiosity.

"What do you mean?" he replied.

"The red and orange paint?"

"You mean the claret and gold? That's my football team colours!"

"Which team?" I enquired in ignorance.

"Motherwell. I've supported them since I was a boy."

"But he's a Dundee United supporter now," quipped Murray McGregor, the assistant Company Secretary. "Though he's wary of displaying their painted colours in Dundee."

Eddie, in his characteristic way blushed and tried to change the subject.

* * *

Having paved the way with Mr Frank, I later made an appointment to look in and have a chat with Peter Philip (son of the Chairman), the catering branch manager.

"Hello Bob," said the polite young Peter as he greeted me. "How are you enjoying life here in W&P?"

"Finding my way around. It's quite a set-up here in Blackness Road: a warehouse, a Cash and Carry depot and your catering branch."

"Our premises here are too small," he told me. "We're hoping to find something bigger soon."

"How many staff do you employ here?

"It's tiny. I have Ian, my office manager, plus a warehouse supervisor, six warehousemen and four drivers."

"What are your main customers?" I asked him.

"Oh, hotels, restaurants, cafes, clubs... We're hoping to get schools someday, but I couldn't cope with that right now."

"How far do your vehicles travel?"

"We deliver all over Dundee, most towns in Angus, and a few in Perthshire and Fife."

This was an impressive range given the resources available. "Sounds like a good coverage. Have you any prospects of a bigger depot?"

"Yes, we are growing quite well. In fact, we have possible plans to move to Invergowrie."

"Really?" I said, nonplussed. "I didn't think Invergowrie would have any warehouse premises."

"There's an amazing old building that was once a meal mill, then a flax spinning mill and later a paper mill that closed about five years ago. It could be developed into a good warehouse with separate goods-in and loading bay areas, and offices too."

"Sounds interesting," I responded. "I hope your plan comes off. Do you have any computer systems to help you?"

"Not really, Bob. I have access to the Central Office computer to print off a profit and loss account, but I'm hoping Mr Frank will get a system for the division someday."

Peter and I chatted about his plans for growth, and it all sounded very positive. He was quite convinced of the catering potential for his branch.

My first year continued successfully – as requested, I had attended both the January and June warehouse stocktakes. They were well organised by Douglas, and I learned that every available male office employee – myself and sales

73

consultants included – were required to assist. The process started after order-picking was complete on the Thursday evening for Friday deliveries, when the bulk stock was taken from around 6pm onwards – up to 10 or 11 pm. The picking lines stock was counted on Fridays, commencing 7 am. It was a learning process, and I was happily included in every stock-take thereafter.

Since returning to Dundee, one matter had occupied my thoughts – reconnecting with my Diploma in Management Studies, which I had commenced at the College of Technology in Bell Street, Dundee (affectionately known as "The Tech") some two years earlier.

In August I set aside the time to make a telephone call to the course leader, as it was important for me to start year three in September. "May I speak with Mr Morrison, please?" I had asked, followed by "Hello is that you Jim?" once the connection had been made.

"Yes," came the reply over the line.

"Bob Murray here. I'm just phoning to ask if I may register for year three of the DMS postgraduate course?"

"Bob Murray from Commercial College?"

"Yes, that's right," I confirmed.

"Where on earth are you?" he asked me.

"I'm in Dundee, and I wondered if I could visit to speak about doing year three, please?" Jim Morrison, I could tell, was quite surprised. After giving him a report on doing year two at Ipswich Civic College, a summary of my last two years and my return to Dundee to work for W&P, he kindly offered me a meeting.

Having the security of Harry's agreement to my continuing the course and obtaining time off work, if required, I was able to accept a place offered by Jim. With two years of

74

study behind me, it was important to finish the course. I would start year three in September.

You're back on track, Murray – off to college yet again.

CHAPTER 7

"Decimalisation Day, February 1971", "Centenary Year", or "Meeting Centenarians"

WORK patterns developed. The division's monthly management meetings continued, the six-monthly stocktake took place in June and Douglas's order pickers, especially new recruits, continued to have occasional training on how to correctly pack unitainers. The most experienced forklift driver was given the task of coaching those drivers who required training. My next priority was to create files for each employee in the division. Meanwhile, various pieces of advice and updates from the government continued to arrive on how to train for UK Decimalisation Day – 15th February 1971.

Daily conversations at the lunch table were varied and gave rise to much excitement – news about Concorde's first supersonic flight and the British and Commonwealth Games came second place to FIFA's football World Cup tournament,

when much heated discussion took place – and it was no surprise that Brazil won the coveted trophy for a third time.

By far the important event for me was a three-day
course in August for Alastair's consultants. After enquiring, I
found that Dundee University provided – during non-term
times – accommodation and training facilities. After making a
few further queries, I was able to secure resident rooms and
training facilities at West Park Hall in the west end of the
city. Charges were minimal, all meals were included and
served, and the peaceful environment was conducive.

Alastair and I discussed the syllabus and, for the first
time, he was able to concentrate in peace and quiet on all the
training ideas he had up his sleeve. Harry was so delighted, he
attended on the last evening to give an encouraging call to the
sales consultants to get out there and break sales records. In
his persuasive style, he had invited Mr Herbert Philip to give
Alastair's team a confidence boost by giving them an insight
into the W&P culture and history.

By his friendly approach and enthusiasm, Herbert had
an infectious impact on the sales team – and chose to give the
company background as a means of saying "anything is possible". His topic was "We are Innovators". He told the story of
Joseph Philip and Thomas Watson, and how the two men had
a strong desire to keep the business within the family.

"Joseph was my grandfather and his son William was
my father, but the interesting thing is that William's sister –
my aunt – married the son of Thomas Watson, whose name
was Preston."

Herbert went on to say how Preston was an industrious and inventive young man who was the first in the country
to experiment with pneumatic tyres using W&P vehicles but,

more than that, he designed and flew the world's first "heavier than air" plane near Invergowrie.

"Gentlemen, the best story I like to share about Preston is that with his analytical mind, he took great care to study the science of flight by leaving the office every lunchtime to walk along Riverside Drive and study seagulls in flight. He was studious and innovative, and was rewarded by flying reputably before the Wright Brothers in 1903."

Preston Watson was accidentally killed in an air crash while training with the Royal Naval Air Force in the South of England. His story is told in Dundee's city museum, and also now included in the city's Transport Museum.

"The strong partnership of the two families has been the driving force within the company," he said. "We started in a small warehouse, and for our first 57 years from 1873 we sold only to catering establishments. In 1930 we moved into supplying the retail grocery trade. At the age of 17 I started off as a salesman, and after three years became head salesman. After the war I began to get involved in developing the company, and we made our first acquisition in 1950 when we took over a grocery wholesaler in Kirkcaldy. The 1950s saw a large increase in grocery retailing. Jim Thomson, one of our managers, warned the company then that cash and carry was going to grow rapidly and seriously injure our delivered trade. It was announced in the local press that C.J. Lang, established grocery wholesalers, was going to open a "Martex" cash and carry in Ward Road, Dundee, and in one week's time would be the first Cash and Carry in the city.

"Do you know what we did, gentlemen? We cleared part of our warehouse, set up our own Cash and Carry, put an advert in the press and beat them by two days. That's what it's about, gentlemen – being alert and quick off the mark. The next year we moved to Blackness Road, created the divisions, bought the foundry premises, and in 1969 we went public with total sales of £12m and net profit of £80k. Here we are, gentlemen, in 1970 approaching £16m sales and net profit of over £280k"

The sales consultants sat mesmerised hearing about Mr Herbert's expert 'hands-on' experiences. After a moment's silence, Harry stood up and asked if there were any questions. Colin, one of the recent starters in Alastair's team, asked "What are the company's next plans for growth?"

Mr Herbert's reply was swift: "We get better at what we do – that's why you are all here this week. And tighter control of our costs – that's why all the budgets you chaps have to adhere to are important."

Jim, another bright consultant, asked him, "What growth is expected?"

"As much as we can grab," was the Chairman's immediate reply, adding, "I have a target for our 100th birthday in 1973 – I'm not allowed to say this publicly, but I can tell you I am looking for over £20m sales and half a million pounds net profit for our big birthday."

It was a glorious end to three days of studying ways and means to grow VG sales, and a wonderful opportunity for the team to hear from the Chairman who spoke with such authority, conviction and ambition. My assessment of it was that Harry had cleverly engineered a memorable moment for Alastair and the sales consultants.

Considering only one or two of those present would have known the Chairman before the start of the evening, they now had a unique experience that few in the division, or perhaps anywhere in the company, could have dreamed of.

The next day Alastair related to me that Donald, a re-cent starter from Glasgow, had innocently asked Mr Philip during the pre-meeting drinks, "And what part of Central Office do you work in?"

Donald now knew!

* * *

My first full year of working in Dundee ended on a high note when, in December, Wendy was christened in Wormit Parish Church. The family were beginning to enjoy the village. The existence of a half crown (12.5 pence) bridge toll was quite a nuisance, but it afforded a quiet peaceful locality.

Meanwhile, work continued to be busy as ever. Discus-sion at the canteen lunch table was gloomy on the first day back at work in January 1971, following the New Year holi-day. The blackest day in Scottish football history, and still to this day in Scotland seen as catastrophic, was the tragic deaths of 66 Rangers supporters at an Old Firm Rangers vs Celtic match when a simple trip by a supporter on an exit from the ground caused a mass pile-up of people. Tales came out for weeks about those who had decided to go to the game at the last minute only to die there, and those who were saved be-cause they changed their mind and didn't attend. Accusations started as to why a previous 'near-bad incident' had not been dealt with.

All eyes were on 15th February 1971 – Decimal Day. The company's decimalisation committee had discussed all aspects involved in financial record-keeping, and all sectors of the company had been represented. Retailers had some dis-quiet about cash handling and of special interest was the ad-aptation of cash registers. The National Cash Register company, with offices and a manufacturing plant in the city, gave assistance. Banks provided me with new coins to enable cash handling exercises with retailers. The explanations were quite straightforward and I wrote up a brief training plan, while Alastair and I decided where and when to run practical training sessions. The word at the time was "familiarity": simply getting used to the new system. We held training sessions in all the usual hotel locations normally used for retailer meetings. There was a genuine need for understanding the new system, and not surprisingly there were many humorous moments – especially when the word 'pennies' was absent-mindedly used instead of 'pence'.

In reality the 'switchover' was almost a non-event, but that was the result of sound preparation. One of the side-effects of decimalisation was price increases. The best example I used to give was that I used to be able to visit my hardware store in Wormit and buy screwnails, individually – say four or six. For the retailer to calculate, in decimals, the price of a hitherto-halfpenny screw was non-sensical, and I found that a new practice was developed whereby a fixed number of screws – perhaps ten or twenty – were now sold in packets for a sum which in reality was somewhere around a 100% or more increase in price. Decimalisation proved to be a bonanza for shops similar to my local hardware store, and it marked the start of more pre-packaging. Not surprisingly, there was no further use for the old penny and threepenny coins which were scrapped. Being left with, say, fourteen unnecessary screws did not go down well with me!

Lunchtime chat began to dwell on upsetting events in the country, with topics ranging from mass protests of tens of thousands of marchers in London and Glasgow against the government's proposals contained in the Industrial Relations

Act through to the prolonged strike by postal workers. Both events took place against the backcloth of the highest unemployment figures in the UK since 1945. Occasionally the UK and EEC discussions for the UK to join the EEC was a brief topic, but with political arguments abounding in the press the subject was wisely and largely avoided at the lunch table.

Later in the year, several events marked some changes in my role. We introduced a brief introductory induction for all new starters, and at the same time started to draft rudimentary job and personnel descriptions for new beginners. When a vacancy cropped up, I decided – in conjunction with managers – to draw up advertisements and in some cases to sit in with a manager at selected interviews. My involvement was growing, and the Training Board claim form began to have more entries with the consequent increase in 'discounts'.

Early in the year, my certificate for completion of year two of my Management Diploma arrived from Ipswich along with hearty congratulations from Colin Dewsbury, the course leader. Only a few weeks later, my membership certificate relating to the Institute of Training Officers arrived. I still have it in a box somewhere, but I was careful not to use the initials within W&P – although, for the record, I did confirm to Harry that I had actually received it. The fixtures in my calendar – stocktaking and retailer meetings around Scotland – also continued.

May of 1971 saw the end of year three of the Management Studies Diploma course. It had been a marathon with year one in Dundee while I was teaching, which now seemed another world behind me, and year two at Ipswich with the kind agreement of The Grocers' Institute when I travelled the 140 miles round-trip to Ipswich Civic College each Wednesday. It was no surprise to find that the relevance of the studies took on a whole new meaning now that I was very firmly in the practical world of management. One subject, organisational structures and management policy, was of particular interest and value, and I was 'blown-over' when I was awarded a commendation which Harry heard about at the prize-giving drinks reception at the end of the course. During the year, on a role-playing negotiating exercise run by the lecturers, I was 'cast' as the trade union representative and it so happened that Jim Morrison took the part of a company manager. I recall the "confrontation" became quite tense and more than heated. At the debrief Jim and his fellow lecturers gave their views and opinions, and it was then that Jim mentioned he didn't enjoy being interrogated by me and thought the play-acting was quite realistic. I thought nothing of it, but he went on to say if there was a prize for the greatest maturity development during the three-year course Bob Murray should receive the award. An amazing comment by Jim, as I had no idea until then just how my work experiences had changed me.

"Was I that timid in year one, Jim?" I responded.

"Let's just say you grew up during the course," he told me.

My own reading of the situation was that I had commenced the course entirely for 'academic' reasons when I taught in the college, but now, I was in a live management world. The course not only enhanced my confidence, but had been hugely relevant. To this day it is the one diploma I treasure most.

Your attention to your studies are paying off. Stick at it!

* * *

During the year I had the idea of introducing a divisional newsletter, the idea being to keep employees up-to-date with company events. I invited employees to submit snippets, and Harry gave me one or two pieces to include. It was named 'WhisPer', with the letters W and P being prominent.

A momentous milestone was reached in August when Carys, now 5 years old, commenced school and happily came home each day with her tin box of new 'flash card words', and soon started to read her first school books.

An announcement was made that the Import Division had made an acquisition. Hitherto, Mr Iain Philip had developed the business organically from within, but in late 1971 the company's first acquisition south of the border made history when an import company based in Liverpool was acquired.

In the later part of 1972, Harry announced at a management meeting that the Board had decided they wanted to recognise the company's one hundredth birthday on 9th June 1973, and requested that managers start to think of ideas of how to mark the occasion. Managers across the company would be asked the same question, and a company committee was to be set up to make recommendations.

In due course the committee met, and I was pleasantly surprised to find that I was included along with Harry, J.B. Thomson and Frank, his Cash and Carry marketing manager. Harry led the group and outlined that we should not only mark the occasion inside the business but to take every opportunity to gain maximum trading advantage in every practical way possible. A long list of ideas was collated and allocated to members of the committee. Trading initiatives had been suggested, and Frank and Jim were left to plan special deals for Cash and Carry customers while Harry instigated similar plans through Alex the buying manager and Alastair the VG sales manager.

One of my ideas was for a special birthday Annual Dinner dance for all Dundee-based employees and managers of each branch or depot around the country. Taking on board the principle that we should try to maximise our trading efforts, I also suggested we try to 'find' as many centenarians in Scotland who shared our birthday year. My idea was that we should write to the readers' column of every daily and weekly newspaper in Scotland seeking the details of centenarians as we wanted to present each with a gift. This would give us 'free' mentions of the company name and business.

Harry also had ideas for a centenary motif to be positioned above every company building and a centenary sticker to be attached to each letter that went out from every office in the company. A suggestion was made by Jim to fly a W&P centenary flag on the Blackness Road buildings. That idea gave rise to some humorous discussion.

Although it was not yet 1973, a great deal of preparation was required by me – newspapers would have to be contacted, a gift for the centenarians would need to be decided upon, and the bigger-than-usual dinner dance had to be planned. By the turn of the year I was ready to put my plans into action. The committee agreed my published letter to go to editors, and after discussion the gift to centenarians was agreed – this was to be a Caithness Glass goblet engraved with both the company and the receiver's name, and a congratulatory message in the form of a one-liner stating "Here's tae us – Wha's like us?". The dinner dance dates and a larger-than-normal venue were agreed and booked, along with a band and a special birthday cake.

Letters along with a completed pro forma questionnaire began to arrive in my office from families in early January, and kick-started a process of communications. It had been agreed that I would visit Registrar House in Edinburgh to confirm dates of birth. Once done, I then had to order appropriately-worded glass goblets from Caithness Glass.

* * *

In addition to the great interest and the emotions of the approaching centenary year was the harsh reality of the introduction of Value Added Tax (VAT) to contend with in April 1973. This was a proposed tax to apply at the point of sale and, as such, it had a particularly important impact on retailers. For one, it would mark the end of Cash and Carry customers paying cash with the resultant no 'accounting profit trail' for the taxman. In future, an invoice would have to be produced by Cash and Carry showing the VAT content in the price. (I recall Jim Thomson tapping his nose when he said all trading was done in cash, with no record of purchases logged.) VAT regulations would end all that freedom. The tax would not apply to all products and would also apply only to businesses over a certain annual turnover figure (I think from memory it was £60k per annum), and so shopkeepers needed to know what the rules would be. In the case of VG retailers who would fall within scope of the new law, Eddie and I decided to hold a Dundee-based one-day training course. We worked together to plan the content. I did all the communicating and Eddie delivered the facts. Based on the success of that course, we expanded the coverage by running evening sessions at the usual retailer meeting venues and went further by offering the course, at a cost, to 'Pinnacle' customers. Eddie's accounting knowledge mastered the intricacies of the legislation and put across a practical guide for attendees. Some VG retailers ran two or three retail units, which underlined how important a topic it was for them. As usual, Eddie and I usually found some humour on our travels. As regards the Pinnacle customers, we hadn't always received confirmation of attendance, and when we arrived in Dunoon we discovered only two retailers had turned up for the course. I had booked a training room which was a lounge in a small hotel. To his great credit, Eddie went through the usual content, and when it was all over we chatted on the way home aboard the McBrayne's steamer about our entire audience.

"First time we've had all our trainees on one settee!" Eddie laughed.

It was all 'go-go-go'!

Your contribution to the business is beginning to kick in – stick at it, Robbie!

* * *

From January 1973 onwards I found myself travelling to places all over Scotland to meet centenarians, and their families, complete with an inscribed goblet which came in a beautiful white silk-lined box. During the year, fifty-four fellow centenarians had been located, and I found myself overawed by the diversity of the men and women I met. Some I visited in their home, others in nursing homes and some in geriatric hospital wards, but mainly at their private residences. Quite a number were still active; I recall a gentleman near Stranraer was still water divining, a lady near Aberdeen found the time and ability to knit, and one or two still enjoyed gardening. Answers as to my question about their longevity were probably predictable: "I never smoked"; "I never drank alcohol"; "I kept myself fit". When I was asked what my observations were about the centenarians I'd visited, I always replied: "They seemed to manage life rather than let life manage them."

They were a marvellous group of people, and I felt honoured to have met so many. Only one passed away before I visited, which left me with an unusual engraved container for pens and pencils on my desk. One story I particularly recall was my visit to a centenarian on the island of Lismore on the West Coast of Scotland. In those days house telephones were rare, and all my communications had to be done by letter. I had no idea of a travel plan other than to drive to the mainland ferry of Port Appin and see what the situation was.

I found the ferry crossing with no problem and, when asked by the ferryman where I was going on the island, he told me I wouldn't need my car as the lady – whom he knew – lived alone only a fifteen minute walk from the quay. "It's the only cottage for miles, ye canna miss it," he had assured me. The lady, a sprightly but slightly stooped, thin person, welcomed me and offered a cup of tea. It was interesting to chat with her about her life and family and, when her cat appeared, I started to speak to it... whereupon she declared in her lilting West Coast tongue: "He'll not be understanding you – he's a Gaelic cat." Amazing! Looking back, I find it quite sad that there was no photographer, newspaper reporter or group of relatives present; just the old lady herself, all alone in her remote cottage.

It was unfortunate that, having made plans to have – for publicity purposes – a local photographer at every presentation, I had not thought it possible to arrange one for that occasion on a far-flung island. (How wrong I had been!) Today I would have had a mobile phone with me, and may have posted the event on Facebook!

A few years later, I met – by accident – the family of a lady in Fife who had received her goblet from me. After chatting for some time, I asked how the lady had enjoyed her special birthday. It was not surprising to learn the centenarian had passed on, but on chatting further about the presentation day the family told me they were saddened she hadn't been fully aware of the reason for my visit.

"Oh, I didn't realise that," I told them. "I'm very sorry about that."

"Don't worry," they responded. "It wasn't a problem; she thought you had come to the house to show her the casket for her ashes!"

That was a good communications lesson for you, Robbie.

"He'll not be understanding you – he's a Gaelic cat!"

My centenarian experiences were captured on Radio Tay when I was interviewed later in the year, and a local item printed in the *Dundee Courier* led to an invitation to speak at a WRI meeting in an Angus village when I gave a twenty minute account of my travels to present birthday goblets. My biggest moment came when I was asked to judge the order of merit for the Homemade Scones competition! Well, perhaps not really – but it felt like it! (Though some expert bakers may have been perplexed at my decision making!)

The centenarian project went very well, and photographs of presentations to recipients appeared in newspapers all over Scotland.

Little could I know, back then, that my mum would herself become a centenarian in December 2014. She was most definitely in the no smoking and no drinking category, and although as a child she suffered rheumatic fever and a weakened heart she was mentally extremely bright and physically energetic up to her last day in April 2015, when she succumbed to a chest infection.

* * *

The usual 150 or so guests at the delivered grocery division's annual dinner dance at the Invercarse became 300, and the event was held in the Angus Hotel, Dundee. Ladies at dinner dances in those days wore long evening dresses and, with a top table featuring the Chairman, all Directors and wives, it was a grand occasion befitting the important milestone in the company's life. Herbert Philip relished the moment and gave a wonderful 'thank you' message to all; it was a captivating, two-way communication event. It was not the moment for him to give a serious financial report, but later that year he was able to state in the year-end accounts that market capitalisation now stood at £1m, being three times the amount shown at the time of the flotation in 1968. Cash and Carry, it was stated, now produced 50% of sales, while delivered grocery and catering produced over a third and the balance filled by Import and the factory. Group employees now totalled over 500.

A near-fire extinguisher moment came when the giant cake – complete with a hundred glowing candles – was briskly wheeled to Mr Herbert's place at the top table, where he took several deep breaths to carry out the ritual. It certainly was a brilliantly bright moment in the company's history.

Do you think you're earning your corn yet, Murray?

Developments were also evident in the catering supply division with the acquisition of Brown's – a wholesale business in Leeds – which J.B. Thomson, with his pioneering skills, had 'found'. His 'scouting' was allowing Frank Keanie to take greater responsibility for the Cash and Carry operation while Jim was seeking further expansion in England. The North Sea oil business was steadily growing, and the Aberdeen catering branch began to seriously turn more attention on supplies to oil companies. Although lucrative, there were some concerns over late payments. Growth was spearheaded by the Branch Manager, Raymond Green, and Charles Philip the Sales Development Manager (son of Iain Philip senior).

The retirement of Mr Frank Philip, Director of Catering, was followed by the appointment of his son Iain as director. Iain had left his business career in South America to take up the position. Peter Philip (son of Herbert) continued in his role as general manager of the Dundee branch. Unfortunately, after only a few months, Iain had to return to Brazil for family reasons. Who would manage the Catering division now?

Charles (son of Mr Iain, the Import Director) was an obvious choice, but he lacked experience. I was asked to have lunch with Charles to ascertain his true feelings for his intended future. When I returned to the board room in the afternoon, I was asked the straight question by Herbert: "Well, Robert?" he said. "Tell us what you found." I was aware of the disappointment my answer would provide.

"Charles is not interested in general management," I replied. "He wants to continue in sales and marketing."

I had never witnessed a high-level business and family disappointment, but I could sense the great sadness that the bright, charismatic, young Charles Philip had innocently inflicted. It seemed inevitable the company would be required to 'look outside' for Frank's successor.

* * *

The special year had added a new dimension and volume to my work, and – with some luck – everything seemed to go off as planned. One highlight for me was that I wrote centre-spread articles for the main national newspapers outlining the attributes of each division, and later learned from Harry that Mr Herbert was evidently "gobsmacked" by the extent of coverage the company enjoyed in the national press.

The idea of a centenary flag never came to fruition – no surprise there!

Shortly after the 'centenary' dust had settled, Harry called me into his office one day and told me my job title was to be changed. Commencing from the next full month, I would be the division's "Personnel and Training Officer". I thanked Harry for the vote of confidence and I was able to respectfully say: "So nothing new there, then."

He laughed and replied, "Well it's now official!"

While we were engaged in the priorities of our hectic grocery distribution world, events in the UK at large were not only distracting but began to have a detrimental influence on employee behaviour and morale. Unsettling events began to drive up discontent. On May 1st 1973 it was reported that 1.6 million workers were on strike protesting against government pay policy. Edward Heath had declared a maximum 7% pay increase should apply, at the same time announcing a 9% increase in National Insurance contributions. Inflation was running at nearly 9%. This was phase 2 of Heath's pay restraint policy and followed on from the introduction of The Industrial Relations Act of 1971, which attempted to control trade unions.

Public disquiet grew not only because of strikes, which heralded a three-day working week, but by IRA bombs exploding at several London Underground railway stations. The 1973 Winter of Discontent had begun. Power supplies were cut. Daily comments regularly included "There's no lighting at home!"; "Rush to buy candles!"; "There's rubbish piled up in streets!" Television footage of out-of-control rats running around bags of refuse in the streets didn't help to improve public morale!

I recall leaving the office with no street lights operating in Dundee, and as I drove across the Tay Road Bridge one evening there was not a single light to be seen in Fife. Such was the desperate plight of households, mum turned up one weekend to gift me a brass paraffin lamp sporting a beautiful canopy. I have not the heart to part with it, and it remains on display in my house as a reminder of her thoughtfulness during those grim winters.

They were difficult and worrying times, and lunchtime canteen chats took on a sombre tone. Pressure was increasing on businesses, and W&P was no exception. Through the Dundee Chamber of Commerce, Mr Hadden had learned that a conference was to be run in London with the topic "Pay Restraint and the Way Forward". Mr Hadden decided that Murray McGregor (Assistant Company Secretary) and I should attend with him. Companies were caught in a tricky balancing act – give in to high pay demands and risk profit drop and the resultant shareholders' alarm, or to find a way to keep employees relatively satisfied. Accounting firms came up with ideas such as 'Profit-Related Pay', which were attempts to find a balancing link between a pay increase with no impact on the 'bottom line'.

You're certainly in the real world now, Murray!

CHAPTER 8

"1974: VG Scotland's 10th Birthday", "1973: Sales Turnover £21m", or "1975: Centra Wholesaler Acquired"

THE Chairman, by the company's 100th birthday, had actually overtaken his targets given at the sales consultants training session by recording sales of £21m and net profit £0.5m.

VG sales were contributing well to the advances, despite growing trends by the national supermarkets. Other competitors were appearing on the horizon in the form of hypermarkets when it was reported in the trade press that a Carrefour hypermarket had opened in Caerphilly, Wales. The feeling, however, was that such giant stores would likely grow only in heavily populated areas.

My range of duties continued, and the personnel content grew with recruitment and selection taking up more of my time. Another celebration soon appeared on the horizon. It was now ten years since Jim Thomson set up the first VG Foodstore in Scotland. Although the franchise areas had been determined by wholesalers throughout the UK, there had been a similar 'sister' development – unrelated in any financial way – with an organisation in Holland called 'VeGe'. I have no evidence that 'VeGe' had any previous influence in setting up VG in the London area, but perhaps Harry had made a connection with that group in the past.

Harry was keen to mark the 10th birthday of VG Scotland and, since Jim had been the leading light, he also had the added desire to see his fellow director recognised for his achievements. Yet another committee – this time of one: Harry himself – suggested to me that he thought it a great opportunity make a trip to Holland and invite our VG retailers to pay their own way for a working conference in Amsterdam.

"If it's a conference, they will be able to claim expenses," he had said. "You can arrange the whole 'caboodle', Bob?"

"Yes, okay, Harry," I'd reassured him. Phew! Hardly under the "personnel and training" title for me but, at a stretch I guess, a few hours of the conference would count as training.

Dates and flights were planned, and I had to make my way to the Apollo Hotel and meet with a VeGe counterpart to set up the itinerary for the trip. After two days I was back in Dundee to discuss flights with travel agents DP&L Travel. Alastair had sent a bulletin to customers to ascertain numbers likely to attend, and it appeared that the most cost-effective method of travel was to fly by a chartered flight from Glasgow. Dates, flight times and a programme of visits to a diamond factory, a coach trip to the Zuyderzee, a sail on a canal boat and an evening out to a typical Dutch restaurant terminating with a gala dinner were all planned. Designated employees including Sales Consultants would attend along with their wives. Eddie and I worked out the costs, and we were able to provide retailers with a price. Suppliers who had helped substantially to finance the trip could also nominate a representative and partner to attend.

Unfortunately (I jest), Eddie and I had to make a trip over to Holland to finalise the programme and make sure our VeGe colleagues had everything confirmed – another opportunity to sample the famous Dutch sailors' tipple: Helvespekel. What a hard life!

Don't kid yourself, Murray. You're enjoying all this travelling!

The Conference was a great success and a relaxing way to form excellent working relationships within the company, and between the company and our customers. Except... Eddie teased me for years afterwards about a humorous occurrence which took place. To travel to the planned evening in a typical Dutch restaurant, two coaches were hired. I was taking the trouble to ensure everyone was on board the coaches, and one retailer's wife mentioned she hadn't seen another couple in our group get on the second coach. I said I'd go and check the first coach and also the hotel lobby. Unfortunately, because of my determined effort to be certain the couple were not left behind in the hotel, I had taken too much care and time in the hotel and the first bus left before I could check it. An assumption was made that I must have got on the first bus, and the second bus drove off without me. Luckily for me, there was a line of taxis at the front door of the hotel, and in the nick of time I was able to gasp an instruction to the Dutch cab driver to "Follow that bus!" Had I not had a glimpse of the bus disappearing around a street corner, I'm pretty certain I would not have had sufficient language skills to explain the address.

* * *

Another FIFA World Cup year came round and helped to add some mock derision and division around the lunch table. Willie Ormond, who was not everyone's favourite, had been scalped by England 5-0 who went on to qualify and had some tough opposition in round one beating Zaire but only drawing with Brazil and Yugoslavia. The canteen was the scene of some anguish about why Ormond didn't push on to grab more goals against Zaire, otherwise Scotland may have advanced to round two. Scotland's attempts, alas, were just not good enough – again! The excitement ended after the final in West Germany, when the host nation beat Holland. There had been ribald jokes and twisted humour – all in the nicest possible way – around the lunch table.

Regrettably there seemed to be a continuing background of strikes and IRA terrorist activities, but we all managed to restrain ourselves from canteen comment – especially when, with a hung Parliament, Harold Wilson became Prime minister when Ted Heath resigned.

Harry and Eddie, realising the increasing competition from other voluntary groups and the impact of supermarkets, decided that more detailed analysis on warehouse and transport systems was necessary. From a list of their priorities, I drew up a job description and personnel profile of what they wanted, and after an advertisement in *The Grocer* magazine Eddie and I travelled to interview a few candidates in Newcastle. Arising from this venture, Dennis, a senior manager within Allied Grocers with work study and cost accounting experience within the distributive grocery trade joined us as Distribution Manager. Douglas could now concentrate on day-to-day "man management", while Dennis would assist Eddie in the policy direction of cost savings and greater efficiencies. Douglas looked in to my office one day to report that his damaged goods problem had been eliminated.

Later in 1974, VG's central marketing team launched a campaign to boost awareness of VG Foodstores. It was to be a nationwide effort with radio, TV and media coverage, and as many opportunities to give VG the greatest possible coverage. The battle between the voluntary groups was fierce, including in-store posters, window displays, and every effort to promote the VG name. The thrust of the activity was to promote the concept of being a convenience store, and the slogan to be featured everywhere was: "VG: Conveniently Yours". This was as much an effort to push the 'convenience' angle, in the face of 'out of town' bigger supermarkets which were an increasing threat.

Each wholesale company was required to send a nominated person to London to be briefed on the many ideas and opportunities that were expected to be applied. Guess who? Yes, it was another one of Harry's nominations from his committee of one. A trip to London in those days meant a car drive to Leuchars airbase near St Andrews in Fife (shared with the military), then a flight to Luton followed by a coach trip to London's West End air terminal. It was a tiring, time-wasteful trip. The project was an interesting one, allowing me to get involved with VG's PR advisor. So although it was diversion from my role, it was an opportunity to learn something about promotions and PR activity from a professional.

* * *

With my Diploma in Management Studies successfully completed, I had been able in recent months to turn my thoughts to commencing a Personnel Management course. For the past winter I'd been attending two evening classes at Dundee Commercial College. I was back in the very college where I had taught retail distribution for five years, but the college – since I had resigned in 1968 – was now housed in a new building at Constitution Hill in the centre of Dundee. In the May of 1975 I sat examinations in statistics, sociology, psychology, economics, training development and industrial relations. It was a return to subjects I'd sat previously, but if I wished to pursue my work in personnel then I must make the effort.

After all the studying you've done, Robbie, this is the one course you must now complete.

Trouble seemed to spark up around that time, mainly in London with protest marches and IRA bombings, but trouble struck nearer home when Harry and his wife were enjoying their summer holiday in 1974. Security and political knowledge must have been lax, allowing him and his wife – and many others – to holiday on the island of Cyprus. We were aware from TV news bulletins that Turkish forces had invaded the holiday resort and were pinning holidaymakers, including Harry, in their rooms for several days. It was a shaken and bemused Harry who returned with tales of 'how close things were'.

Many years later I found myself on a walking holiday in North Cyprus, and was able to visit the deserted 'hideaway' luxury bungalow where Lt. Georgios Grivas had his remote base where, I was told, he received shipped arms to help overthrow Archbishop Makarios as part of his aim to unite

Cyprus with Greece and from where he conducted his clandestine communications. The bullet-ridden hotels in the coastal South Region of the island were still plain to see. It was only then I had some sense of the danger Harry and his wife must have experienced.

In September, I found myself most definitely involved in Personnel and training duties when the company acquired Peek, Winch and Todd Ltd. – a wholesale grocery company which distributed to small retailers as well as larger retail businesses operating under the Centra group label. The company had depots in East Kilbride and at Newbridge, near Edinburgh. It was all hands on deck to take stock at both depots, and Eddie and I travelled to each of the sites in one day to double-check the counts and to give me the opportunity to interview staff.

The arrival of Centra brought with it the need to visit the depot regularly and develop sound working relationship with both managers. My personnel procedures had to be introduced, and this was highlighted as being crucial when one day Bill the depot manager was visited by the police who came to ask questions about one of his truck drivers. Evidently the driver had been under surveillance for some time, and it was discovered he had posted dynamite from a small post office near Livingston to an address in Northern Ireland. Bill was shaken by the discovery, and we all realised we had to be vigilant.

Around the same time, W&P acquired the Turriff depot from Hutcheons who also operated under the Centra banner. After assessing the needs of the new business, Dennis was involved in recommending operational changes while I was attending to consequential redundancies. It was a first major acquisition by Eddie, and began a process of integrating and developing new business.

Good progress, Robbie – and you're learning as you go!

* * *

Forever on the lookout to advance and enhance the VG brand, Eddie in 1975 convinced Harry to offer a conference to VG retailers to Majorca. I'm not sure what sparked this initiative; perhaps the success of the trip and conference in Amsterdam encouraged him, or possibly the notion that other VG wholesalers in the UK were doing something similar.

"Bob, I want to take our VG retailers to Majorca for a conference," he stated. "Holland went well, so can you fix it for me?"

"Sure, Eddie; just say what you want. But what's the budget?" I asked.

"It'll be the same as before – wives included, and retailers pay their flight. Suppliers will contribute, and you'll fix up an itinerary for a week."

With the steady advance of writing personnel procedures and dealing with recruitment at more depots, I remember wondering if I was spending my company time to greatest advantage. On this occasion I did not have the luxury of assistance from VeGe personnel as I had in Holland; this was a step into the unknown. Somehow, I contacted Martin the manager at DP&L Travel Dundee with the prospect of booking a holiday for a large group. He fixed up accommodation for myself in the Santa Ponsa Park Hotel, Santa Ponsa, in order that I could meet hotel management. It seems now to be shrouded in the mists of Majorca, but I managed to set up a week's standard holiday for retailers with the extra cost of a

Gala dinner on the last evening – much to the monetary delight of the hotel manager. With the help of hotel management and a conference executive, I was able to visit places of interest and build up a plan of accommodation and day trips to the Soller Mountain Railway, the Caves of Drach, and a coach trip to the mountains. Included was a typical Spanish variety show and a trip to the inevitable wine and sherry-tasting afternoon.

Eddie was delighted with the plan, and set about finalising the costs and the funding he needed from suppliers to cover their own cost and that of W&P managers and wives. Persuasion and a free trip for suppliers' reps encouraged companies to provide Eddie with funds. For Eddie, it was a show case product for his customers – not forgetting the enticement for Centra retailers who were now aboard. Harry and his wife were also included.

My efforts were to supervise the entire trip, making especially sure that we lost no one. Luckily everyone came home in one piece and raved about having had a great trip. I still have the Spanish pottery bowl gifted to me by retailers at the gala dinner – it sits alongside the windmill-decorated Dutch beer jug I was presented with in Amsterdam.

* * *

When Harry had earlier seen the need to add strength to the distribution department, a similar assessment was applied by him to the sales area and – through his contacts – an experienced manager, to whom Alastair would report, with wide knowledge of voluntary group development in England was appointed. This prompted Alistair regrettably to leave W&P, and seek what turned out to be a successful career in food distribution in Zambia. It was my first loss of a highly supportive manager with great enthusiasm, and a sad loss for the team. Alistair had been a keen apprentice of Jim Thomson, and it was my first harsh reality lesson of facing the loss of a highly respected colleague. Collateral damage, one might say, on the road of progress. It was a shame especially that, in time, the 'highly recommended' newcomer did not 'cut the mustard' and didn't last long. Harry was let down badly. Eddie was never impressed by the newcomer who, on a stock-taking early morning, played a silly prank on Eddie by moving forward by one hour the hands of Eddie's office wall clock. This strategy was not in Dale Carnegie's book *How to Win Friends and Influence People.*

Replacing Alistair was Jimmy Harper, who had joined the division as a sales consultant for the Dundee and Angus area in 1973 when he advised over forty retailers. Having been promoted to VG Sales Manager, North Scotland, in 1974, he was handed the task of nurturing the newly acquired Centra business for all of Scotland under the title of General Sales Manager. His priority was to assess the Centra sales potential while Dennis studied the opportunities and savings regarding operations.

Eddie was in full flight now, and given the successful build of greater customer loyalty with the VG Majorca conference he did not surprise me one day when he announced his plan for a Centra conference morale booster in November. Guess where... and guess who would arrange? No need to say anything further. It was a great success, spoiled at the end only by the news from home that a snow storm had hit Scotland and resulted in a limited number of retailers (including Eddie and his wife) being allowed to board the last flight out of Majorca which would land at Edinburgh. I dare not think now what the criteria was for selection on the Edinburgh flight, but the remainder of us – including Jimmy Harper – suffered a flight to London followed by a slow rail journey from London to Edinburgh. I've no recollection of how we all found our way to the car park at Edinburgh Airport and then drove back to Dundee.

Ultimately it was no surprise that the 'best' Centra accounts were transferred to VG and serviced from Dundee. A process of transfer and closure then took place – remaining East Kilbride accounts were transferred to Newbridge, followed – in time – by moving all Newbridge accounts to Dundee. Obviously, redundancies fell under my responsibility. It was always unfortunate to damage peoples' lives, and I always delivered the 'line' to employees that, "yes, one door has closed, but perhaps a more interesting door may open." Easy for me to say while sitting on the 'safe' side of the table.

I recall having an impromptu chat with Jimmy one day outside my office door. "How are you coping with all those changes, Jimmy?" I asked him.

"Been hectic," he admitted, "but I'm glad to be based in Dundee again with a wider remit as VG Sales Manager, Scotland." Jim's experience was quite typical of the period, with ongoing change and growth.

"Are you pleased with those developments, Eddie?" I enquired of him one day.

"It's growth, but we need profit – wait and see!" This was typical of his positive cautionary approach.

* * *

Harry called me into his office one day and asked if I would kindly consider helping him out by offering to chair the Training Committee of the Wholesale Grocers' Association of Scotland (WGAS). His angle, which I couldn't dismiss, was that if I was Chair and adviser on the committee then I would be in a position to run training courses across Scotland by securing participants from other wholesale association members. This was of immediate appeal, as I had been thinking for some time of attracting course organisers, but had lacked sufficient numbers from within W&P. The Association employed only one full-time administration manager/secretary, and luckily for me this post was held by the enthusiastic Kate Salmon who generated great support.

Little did I realise this was the start of an ongoing programme of appropriate courses for the trade in Scotland. Yet again, those enlightening moments had their downside (I jest once more), as each year I was obliged to attend the Association's annual conference, dinner and dance in venues, typically Peebles Hydro or Dunblane Hydro. "Life's just not fair!" I would often say to Harry.

While chatting with Dennis one day, I learned he was planning a visit to Turriff to tie up some loose ends. As I too had reason to be there to deal with redundancies, we decided to drive together in his car. "How is your transfer of accounts coming on, Dennis?" I asked him.

"Going well, Bob," he replied confidently.

"Will the benefits show through?"

"Oh yes, there's no doubt. W&P are in the forefront of business consolidation within the trade. All franchises are contracting as the multiples rapidly expand with bigger and better stores."

"Are our recent acquisitions typical of what you were seeing down south?"

"Yes, our recent buy-out of Ritchie's A&O franchise business in Dundee is a good example, and of course we also gained when we transferred business from Mutch of Elgin into Turriff depot. Such was the speed of advance, Mutch lost twenty-seven retail customers when Fine Fare opened a new out-of-town supermarket."

"What's the latest news on our talks with the Peterhead wholesaler that Harry's so keen to acquire?"

"That's a joke," Dennis snorted. "I believe the wholesaler took so long to make up his mind that he went out of business. Just indicates the rapid pace of change."

"Yes, we need the volume to survive ourselves," I observed.

"Exactly. We need to continue putting more business through Blackness Road."

"I wouldn't be surprised if Eddie and Harry try to go for the big one at Aberdeen."

"Oh, you mean G&P merchants? I'm sure that's on a list," Dennis told me.

* * *

Amongst the redundancies, recruitment, training and arranging or attending meetings, foreign and otherwise, there came along some light moments. One such evening was the annual Boxing Dinner, in the city's Angus Hotel, featuring St Francis – the well-known Dundee amateur boxing club.

Harry and J.B. were joint sponsors of a W&P table, and in addition to some selected suppliers' reps a few of my management colleagues were there including Frank, J.B.'s marketing manager. It was a fascinating and bizarre experience – enjoying some delicious food while two young boxers were 'hammering' each other in the ring only a few feet away and providing the occasional spray of boxers' fresh blood landing on the lily-white table-cloth. Once the bountiful supply of drinks began to take effect, the support and side-betting began, and so too did the volume of encouragement – enough to raise the roof. Eddie at one point raised alarm by loudly reporting that some spots of blood had landed on his plate of Beef Bourguignon.

During an interval between bouts, and during those days of unrestricted smoking in such gatherings, it was common for cigarettes and cigars to be liberally offered. A scantily-clad young lady approached our table offering cigars. With Harry's words echoing in my ears to 'look after' our supplier guests, I indicated to each of my fellow diners to take a cigar from the box as it circled the table of a dozen merry guests. To my amazement, no one took up my kind offer, and so – believing they were part of the 'package' on offer – took one of them myself. Then the young temptress declared, "That'll be £12!" I was never a big spender at the company's expense, but my carefree attitude on that occasion could have cost Harry £144 – approximately two months' pay for a lorry driver! Eddie teased me for many days about my 'dice with death' with over-spending, as Harry would eventually spot my over indulgence on checking the bills for the evening. Such events were part of the rich strands of fun that were woven into the hard long hours we all put in to working for our company.

An everlasting image I still recall to this day was that, at the end of the evening as we were making our way out of the hotel along a wide corridor, we saw two boxers – now dressed smartly – being photographed sporting facial cuts and bruises, grinning from ear to ear with an arm over each other's shoulder, having been only an hour or so earlier seriously fighting each other with gusto.

Some time later, the acquisition of D McDiarmid & Son (Perth) resulted in the merger of that business with the Dundee catering branch, and the Invergowrie former mill premises (on which Peter Philip had long set his sights) became the enlarged 9,000 square feet Dundee branch – albeit initially with Portacabins as offices. I visited Ian Dutch at Invergowrie, and he gave me the run-down on his new, enlarged business.

"Like all branch managers, I'm responsible for sales, margin, gross profit, expense control and return on capital," he told me. "I now have six delivery vehicles and twenty-six employees covering warehouse, drivers, buyers, and office staff and sales reps."

"You've grown quite a bit," I remarked. "What is the customer situation nowadays?"

"We have around 600 customers – and, in addition to the usual range of businesses, we now supply universities, schools and off-shore rigs and platforms. We cover Dundee, Angus and all Perthshire and North East Fife."

Ian showed me around the depot, which was a good example of how the catering business was expanding – yet still following the company's policy of low-cost premises. "Great progress, Ian," I told him. "I wish you all the best."

CHAPTER 9

"Herbert Philip Retires", or "Promotions and Boardroom Changes"

THE year 1976 began with animated chat at the lunch table about supersonic Concorde's first commercial flight from London to Bahrain and how, theoretically, we could fly to Spain on holiday in about half an hour. The chat was accompanied with some wry comments and leg pulling about even easier trips to VG and Centra conferences – especially by those around the table who didn't participate!

After many years as Chairman and Chief Executive, Herbert Philip decided to retire. He had seen massive change and diversification during his tenure. He had streamlined the management structure and, in particular, had recognised the need for strict budgetary controls. He had been a charismatic figure with a dynamic approach.

The role of Chairman was now split, and Mr D.C. Greig, a non-executive director, became the company's first non-executive Chairman, while Harry Gardner was appointed Group Managing Director. Coincidently, J.B. Thomson – the pioneer VG veteran, and latterly director of Cash and Carry – had also decided to retire. He would be sorely missed, as it was through his undoubted 'all round spearheading' skills while seconded to Catering division that he was instrumental in 'finding' Browns catering business in Leeds. In a rather strange twist of events, his lookalike Sid James was in the news when he died around the same time that Jim commenced his well-earned retirement.

Herbert's decision created fundamental changes across the group. Eddie, Operations Manager in Delivered Grocery, was appointed a main board Director with total responsibility for the division, while Frank Keanie – J.B. Thomson's energetic and influential marketing manager – was likewise appointed main board director with responsibility for Cash and Carry division.

My workload by this time consisted of divisional personnel and training matters along with local surveys of employee benefits, the Wholesale Grocers' training committee, and the recent need to prepare reports for our company lawyer to present our cases at Industrial Tribunals – not forgetting my occasional straying into PR and Customer Relations initiatives launched by Harry.

Around this time was a customer relations event, when I was asked to accompany two top winners of a VG UK golf tournament held at Carnoustie. The two winners qualified to play in the final at St Pierre Golf Club, near Chepstow, South Wales. "You come from Carnoustie, Bob. You are exactly the person to accompany our two winners!" Harry had suggested.

As it happened, I did know both finalists – Ron Beatt from Newport in Fife, as we had travelled together to London in 1959 to sit our Grocers' Institute exams, and I had helped with training the other winner – VG shops owner Harry Lawson from Broughty Ferry, Dundee. "Yes, I know both winners, Harry," I confirmed, "but I can't play golf now – well, to be honest, I never could."

"Just go and check out their bunkerrrrrrs," he'd replied in his pseudo-Scottish fun tongue. "You never know what you might find."

My memory of the trip is certainly not of my golf, but rather of a strange encounter. Not surprisingly, I had hit a shot away off target. When I went to play my ball in a deep bunker, and to apologise to the green keeper who was actually working in it, I was staggered when he said, "That wasn't one of your best shots I've seen, Robert!"

Probably looking stunned, I managed to blurt out, "Stewart?"

"That wasn't one of your best shots I've seen, Robert!"

"Yes, it's me," he smiled. "How's your mum these days?"

"Goodness me! Stewart Christie!" Stewart had lived across the street from my parents in Carnoustie. We chatted for a couple of minutes, and I learned that he had worked at St Pierre for a few years. "Course is looking well," I told him.

"Aye, thanks," he replied with a grin. "I learned all that in Carnoustie. "

We chatted for a further few minutes until I heard my partners calling me on. Meeting Stewart was a wonderful moment, and a reminder just how much the golf courses at Carnoustie act as a training ground for green keepers to use their talents around the world.

When I returned from Chepstow, I found a note on my desk from Harry asking me to look in to speak with him. "Good morning," he greeted me as I entered his office. "How did it go?"

I told him it was a very long drive ("and I'm not talking golf"), but a pleasant day – and I had met a Carnoustie green keeper while I was there. "I did say you may find something interesting in St Pierre bunkers," Harry reminded me. "Anyway, I have some news for you."

"Ah," I said with some trepidation. "Is that good or bad news?"

"That depends on you. You know that Herbert has retired? Well, you're still going to report to me, but now as Group Personnel Manager."

"Oh?"

"Yes, as you know I'm now Group MD, and I'll be based in Central Office – and so will you."

It took my breath away but I quickly saw the scope of working for Harry in a wider group scale.

"When does it start, Harry?" I asked him.

"There's a bit to do. First of all, there needs to be a few communications, so say nothing about this yet. But Eddie knows about your move, so you can speak with him. Eddie will move in to this office in due course."

My world suddenly opened up. No more stock-takes for Eddie. I'll be in Central Office, and I'll be reporting to Eddie for Delivered Grocery, Frank for Cash and Carry, Mr Hadden for Central Office, and to the recently-appointed Catering Director, David Shentall. In fact, the W&P world would look quite different with a new-look board of directors. I'd never reported to J.B., but the younger directors were in my age bracket and it all seemed comfortable. What was most agreeable was that Harry wanted me to remain reporting to him.

My immediate thought was to take time to make a plan to visit each Divisional Director to ascertain priorities and set up a programme visits to each location. In a matter of days, Harry was installed in Central Office which was now accommodated in an expanded area within the Blackness Road complex. The boardroom would now double-up as his office. Harry's brief to me was simple: "Just do for the divisions what you've done for me in Delivered Grocery, Bob."

"That sounds good, Harry. Will that mean conferences abroad for all Divisions now, and more PR involvement?"

"These were all Delivered Grocery promotional ideas. You won't have time for that sort of stuff now," he explained. "Just set up the basics as you've done for me."

The message was clear. Concentrate on the divisions' priority personnel and training issues.

Robbie, do you remember the advice you got all those years ago from John Simpson, the Training Director at the

Grocers' Institute: training will open the door into personnel management? Well, you're there now!

* * *

Since Delivered Grocery was my 'homeland', I decided my first divisional meeting should be with Eddie, who was now set up in Harry's old office. When I entered the large, square, wood-panelled, carpeted office – complete with expensive-looking, 'non-football green' – curtains, Eddie was busy moving an extraordinarily high 'tower' of document trays in different spots on the front of his desk. He sat in his new high-back swivel chair and asked Ann, his secretary – who was now installed in the same office – to stand at the door. "Can you see me from that angle, Ann?" he asked her.

"No, Mr Thompson," she replied.

"Is that some kind of psychological trick Eddie?" I asked him good-naturedly.

He blushed in his characteristic style with a smile on his face. "No, I just like it like that, Bob."

I was intrigued by Eddie's thinking, as I recalled seeing a similar arrangement when I first met him. Did he like to hide behind trays? And, if so, for what reason?

"Congratulations on your appointment Eddie," I told him. "I wish you all success."

"Thanks, Bob. We'll still be working together."

Changing the subject, I mentioned to Eddie a piece of history I had only recently learned. "This is a famous office, Eddie, and that window behind you is even more historic."

"Oh, really, Bob?" he asked wonderingly. "And why's that?"

"During Churchill's campaigning visit to Dundee in May 1908, he addressed his followers – who had gathered in Blackness Road – from that open window."

"Did he really?"

"So I believe, Eddie. But his political address was intentionally disrupted by a group of suffragettes, led by Mary Malone, who came charging down the road on a barrow and clanging a loud bell."

"Well, I won't be making any speeches from that window, Bob," he assured me with a wry smile.

"And hopefully there'll be no suffragettes either – but you never know, Eddie; you may want to give a speech when you become Chairman of the company."

Eddie batted off my comment with his characteristic mixture of humour, intensity and determined business focus. He was not the kind of man to be swayed by frivolity, but he enjoyed light-hearted moments. We were quite alike in that respect. We shared a relaxed and humorous professional relationship, but we each knew what the other wanted and I admired his no-nonsense, efficient and effective management style.

With the number of events I shared with Eddie during company conferences and social events arranged within the company, I found that it was comfortable for our respective families to share private time. Both Eddie and I had children of a similar age, and we found ourselves arranging birthday or Christmas parties together. I can still picture young Stephen playing with his Christmas gift Subbuteo on my lounge floor.

* * *

In early 1977 I received word that I had passed my personnel exams, and my certificate from the Institute of Personnel Management (IPM) arrived confirming at the same time that I was now an Associate Member. All very helpful, but something I didn't mention in my work context – unlike my college days, when initials after one's name was actively encouraged. Initials after my name would have sent out the wrong signals.

It's been a long and busy road, Murray. John Simpson always said the Personnel Manager's light was always the last one to be switched off at night.

Lunchtime chats gave rise to a mixture of reportable events. One or two colleagues had won money by betting on Grand National winner Red Rum, while later in the year Kenny Dalgleish's transfer from Celtic to Liverpool livened up debate. I'd seen him play at Dens Park in Dundee, and there was no doubting the way he dominated the game with his superb skills. Along with these light-hearted moments there was sadly no way of escaping the country's dire problems of unrest which had dominated UK life for the past few years. If anything, it seemed to worsen each year. One of the most disturbing cases was the strike of London undertakers, resulting in 800 bodies lying in wait of burial.

Despite the continuing gloomy political and economic troubles in the country, in 1978 the divisions were making remarkable progress. With inflation running at over 8% and with unemployment at a new high of 1.5 million, strikes were commonplace which resulted in major disruption. Industrial disputes closed down *The Times* newspaper business for a period, and panic buying of bread resulted from a British Bakeries strike. Low morale in the country at large was evident, and made worse by the fact that near the end of 1978 the BBC was taken off the air for two days.

My delivered grocery priorities outlined by Eddie were to work with Dennis on improving warehouse and transport operations. Dennis was well on top of matters, and my only involvement was to assist him and Douglas in recruiting. Disciplinary matters took up some of my time, but now that Centra business was fully integrated into the Blackness Road warehouse less travel to depots was required. "I'm putting out a note to all managers to say that they must contact you whenever recruitment advertising or disciplinary help is needed," Eddie told me.

"That's perfect, Eddie," I responded. "I'll continue with all the help I've been giving you – nothing will change."

"You'll still come to my managers' meetings Bob. I want you to know what's going on. But not the budget meetings. You'll be on a Central Office budget now, so no more stocktakes."

Forever sharp on costs, Eddie asked me about my secretarial help. "You'll no longer need any help from Delivered Grocery?"

It was more a statement than a question, but luckily I was able to confirm that I'd be required to recruit a secretary with costs related to Central Office.

While benefiting from Eddie's pool of secretaries, I had never had to consider the costs of a secretary nor the cost of equipment. But now I was permitted to recruit a secretary. When I engaged Nan and discussed office space and equipment with her, I ran into the thorny questions of typewriters. I discovered there was quite some rivalry between secretaries in those days about who had the best typewriter. It seems ludicrous today, in the world of word processors, that such jealousies existed. When I asked Nan what typewriter she had been using in her previous job, she told me, "It was a 'golf ball head' machine. I hope I can have one here," she had added innocently.

Finding myself speaking with other managers, I discovered there was a range of machines and prices. I wasn't much different from Eddie in respect of keeping costs down, and consequently I had to do some research.

"What was the manufacturer?" I asked Nan.

"It was an IBM Scelectric," she replied.

"And what is a golf ball head then, Nan?" I enquired. "Why is it important to you?"

"Instead of the usual 'basket' of individual keys that engage with the paper, a 'golf ball' (or should I say a 'type-ball') is more efficient and less noisy."

"I'll need to check with managers in Central Office and find out what machines other secretaries are supplied with."

When I made enquiries, I found managers were unaware of details and invited me to speak directly with secretaries. Information was varied – some ladies used Olivetti, Underwood or Remington typewriters. When I began asking about 'golf ball heads', I received 'hurt' replies which indicated they were not in that elite bracket. It was a new world to me, but I gathered some were using manual machines with either correcting papers or ribbons, and some were using machines which required the use of 'Tippex'. I had to hear all about the problems of the Gestener copier machine, and of the frequent problems between typists about not putting the lid back on the bottles of Tippex fluid!

It was a baffling world for me, but more alarmingly I discovered there was a hierarchy at work – the more senior the manager they were working for, the better the typewriter. When I finally spoke with a director's secretary and mentioned Nan was looking for a 'golf ball head' machine, it was as if the world had come to an end. "Oh no," she told me, "I'm the most senior secretary here, and I'm the only one with a golf ball head."

When I had to trouble Harry with this silly situation, he shook his head and advised me to wait till he would speak to her later. Obviously some sensitive questions must have been asked, but word came back in due course that the secretaries with non-electric machines would ultimately move on to electric equipment and that the quantity of my work would justify the spend on a golf ball head.

I had never come across any managers pushing 'rank', but it was an enlightening insight for me into the sensitive world of typists. It wasn't long until, in the 1980s, word processors were introduced – but I then heard about the problems of copiers and printers! By that point, health and safety had raised its head, and it was instructed that female word processors must wear a protective apron – especially if they were pregnant. The forgotten 'typist world' of the 1970s and 80s!

* * *

On one visit to Dennis's office, I asked him what were his main issues. His professional expertise was evident. "My main efforts are for us to become more efficient by introducing work study-based incentive schemes in the warehouse and on the transport side," he explained. "Because of limitations of coping with bigger vehicles in our restricted workshop, I am looking at bringing in 'demountable body' lorries to increase capacity. Our man Frank, the workshop foreman, does a great job – he's saving us two vehicles with his ongoing maintenance programme. The legal requirements of the Operator's licence are being more severely enforced, and his preventative maintenance works well."

"What changes do you envisage in the warehouse, Dennis?" I prompted him.

"There's good news there, because Lansing Bagnall are prepared to give free training and certificate forklift truck drivers – providing we use their trucks across the company."

"Can the same happen with lorry driver training?"

"Oh yes; if we replace trucks with 'Mercs', we'll get free driver training. Mercedes would also provide stats on vehicle running costs. Eddie likes that idea, as it will cut costs and help our budgeting." This was proof that Eddie's appointment of Dennis was providing new ideas and new solutions.

Meanwhile, VG sales were making ground, and the integration of selective A&O and Centra retailers meant that overall accounts being serviced from Blackness Road had increased from around 150 to over 300. Things were buzzing!

My first meeting with Frank, the newly-appointed, marketing-orientated Director of Cash and Carry, got off to a positive start. Frank explained that although business was going well, his depot managers needed help as growth continued. He wanted me to start visiting depots on a regular basis and also be ready to dash off to help resolve any staffing problems. There had been one or two examples of 'untidy' employee dismissals, and Frank wanted me to be involved at an earlier stage. Effectively he wanted his managers to contact me in order that staff problems could be 'nipped in the bud', as he put it. He also wanted me to get involved in recruitment advertising.

"I don't want regular reports, Bob," he told me, "but keep me in the picture whenever you deem it necessary. You'll now sit in on my managers' meetings so you'll hear what's going on."

Depots were located at Dundee, Clydebank, Kilmarnock, Kirkcaldy, Paisley and Greenock. I liked Frank's open, positive and gregarious attitude, and I could see how his managers readily responded favourably to his leadership style.

* * *

"Come in, Mr Murray," I could hear David Shentall say after I knocked on his office door. He was expecting me. "Congratulations on your appointment, Bob," he told me as I walked into the office.

"Thanks, David. I hope I can be of some help. How are you settling in to life here in Bonnie Scotland?" I asked him.

"Very well, thanks. I've been getting around the country quite a bit, and enjoying the travelling a lot more here."

David had been known by Harry from previous VG grocery distribution success, and had moved his family to live near Dundee. I had first met him at a Heathrow hotel when the "VG: Conveniently Yours" advertising campaign was launched, and I had asked him what part of England he had originated from.

"What's the town in England with a twisted church spire?" he had enquired of me in response.

"Tell me."

"Chesterfield. That's my native heath, and that's the football team I support too!" he added as he shook a small phial containing what must have been Angustura Bitters into his double gin and replaced the tiny bottle in his waistcoat pocket.

"Great! I'll watch their progress from now on," I told him. We chatted for a few minutes, and then I asked: "How can I be of any help to you and the Division?"

"That's a tricky one. You probably know Frank Philip never brought his managers together, so you won't be required to attend any meetings. But I would like you to start visiting branches and implementing your procedures. In due course I'm going to change the culture and get cross fertilisation."

"I understand," I nodded.

"Meantime, my priority is to develop a brand image for the division."

"What form will that take, David?"

"I'm going to launch 'Cater Care', with a recognisable symbol and logo.

"Is there any priority for my visits to branches?" I enquired.

"No, none at all. At present we have branches at Dundee, Edinburgh (Newhaven), Glasgow, Leeds and Aberdeen. As I've said, they run the show at the moment, entirely without my close involvement."

"Raymond has left us now and Charles Philip has been pressed to run the Branch," I observed. "Raymond was a great operator and Charles, as you know, prefers the selling side of the business."

"Yes, Raymond was quite a character. He will be hugely missed. Did you ever hear how he started work with W&P?" David asked me.

"No, don't think so."

"The story which picked him out as a determined man is how he convinced Herbert he was the person for the job. I'm told that on his demob in 1945, he turned up at the branch office to be interviewed by Herbert and claimed he was an experienced salesman. He convinced Herbert he had a driving licence, got the job and the car, but had never driven in his life. He spent the weekend reading a manual about driving, picked up the car on Monday and drove around the city all day to get used to the vehicle. I'm told he was a shrewd and successful manager.

"Once you have visited all the branches, come back and give me your views," he said. "John McGill at Glasgow, like Raymond, is an experienced operator, and Joe McNamara – the manager at Edinburgh – is of a similar style. At Invergowrie we have a young man who was office manager when young Peter Philip (Herbert's son) managed the Branch. Peter has left the company to do his own thing – always a shame when a youngster doesn't want to follow in his dad's footsteps. So young Ian Dutch is relatively new to management, and is doing a really good job."

"What are the other directors saying to you?" David asked me. Referring briefly to my chats with Frank and Eddie, I gave him a sense of how things were being viewed. "That sounds fine to me. Do we meet regularly, Bob?"

"Yes, I'll keep you posted on events. With a once-a-month meeting, if you want."

And that was it: I was left to plough my own furrows It seemed quite different from the other two operating divisions, but I realised I must not be too much of a 'new broom' and that I should tread carefully and helpfully.

* * *

Before I had a chance to call on Mr Hadden, he phoned and asked if I would look in to see him. In his own inquisitive and professional way, he asked me to relate how my meetings with directors had gone and how the agendas were shaping up. He was content with my approach, and went on to say he would let me know if and when he needed my help – making it clear at the same time that I should let him know if I should encounter any serious problems in any of the divisions. His guidance was valuable, and I was aware that he wanted to keep an eye on my entire activities – perhaps to gauge if the investment in me was being justified, and maybe also to have an insight into the recently-appointed directors. In short, I picked up the point that he wanted to know only of significant matters and not to report unless deemed important.

I took the opportunity to raise with him a timely question I had, and I set the scene: "There have been a few recent unfair dismissal claims by employees and, as you probably know, I was guided by Harry to use our company lawyers to fight them at industrial tribunals."

"What's the problem then?" Mr Hadden questioned.

"Well, we have won several cases, but we lost one that we should have won."

"So?"

"It's costing us big money, Mr Hadden, to win or lose – and I think I would have won the case we lost."

"What difference could you have made?"

"As you know, the tribunal comprises of a legally qualified Chairperson, a representative of an Employers' Association, and a member of a TUC-affiliated Trade Union. I think we lost our case because we were caught up in a legal wrangle when I think I could have convinced the two representatives on the tribunal to see a down-to-earth management situation."

Mr Hadden didn't seem entirely convinced. "That's pretty bold, Bob, is it not?"

"I realise you won't want to upset our company law-yers (a well-known, long-established firm in the city) by ex-cluding them, but I think I can make savings."

"Lawyers will have sufficient work from us without worrying about losing income from tribunals," he remarked.

"If a straightforward case comes up, I'm willing to have a go at handling it. I've seen how the procedures work. By the time I brief our lawyers, I'm well acquainted with all the facts. In any case, with my closer supervision of all disciplinary actions by managers there should be fewer tribunals. It's bet-ter than paying around £1,000 each time we hire a lawyer."

"Okay then: give it a try," Mr Hadden acknowledged. "Let me know how it goes."

Don't get too cocky, Murray – remember, don't rush in. That was Mr Hadden's first piece of advice to you.

"By the way, we are continuing to grow," he added. "I'm recruiting a financial accountant to 'beef up' the function in Central Office. I know what I'm looking for, but I'll let you know if I need your help."

A new scene was set for me: a close connection with every location manager across the whole company. I would implement my procedures and policies, and develop new ones as I go. This was a major step forward I could now start to build up a company-wide manual of personnel and training policies and practices.

Lunchtime chats had been lively and emotional for sev-eral months leading up to Scotland's qualification to play in the FIFA World Cup held in South America. It was the hal-cyon days of Ally McLeod, who steered the team.

Eddie invited me to join him and friends to watch the opening game at his home. It was a stirring evening. The press had us believing we could easily win. We were going to take on the world... but alas, in that first game Peru beat us 3-1. We all had our views about why we didn't beat Iran, and the game against the Netherlands was hotly debated – especially Archie Gemmill's brilliant goal which commentators said at the time was one of the greatest individual goals ever scored in a World Cup tournament.

CHAPTER 10

"The 1980s and Britain's Problems", or "Ian Macpherson Joins the Company"

HAVING peaked in 1977, the company's profits began to dip. In an effort to stave off the downward turn, Harry attempted to diversify by entering the self-drive car and van hire business sector.

The autumn of 1978 saw renewed troubles in the UK, with a combination of social and economic problems and uncertain political direction. The second 'Winter of Discontent' had begun. In the early part of 1979, rail workers went on a succession of 24-hour strikes and lorry drivers across the country joined them in their industrial action. Such damaging actions seemed to be everywhere, with thousands of schools closed due to lack of coal for heating while tens of thousands of public service workers withdrew their labour, resulting in no street cleaning and no collection of garbage. Parks and grass verges were left unattended. It was described at the time as the worst level of unemployment since the general strike of 1926. Later in the year the ITV network was closed down by strikes and in August, to add to the misery of the population, Lord Mountbatten was murdered by more IRA action.

Curiously, work continued for me more or less as normal and W&P did not appear to suffer seriously from a trading or sales point of view, although profits continued to slip. We did have a bad reaction from our lorry drivers when the annual pay review came up for discussion in April. The government had stated strict limitations on pay awards to curb inflation, and this angered our drivers. Eddie had to meet with the workers and came back to report to me that one of their observations was that "Bob Murray's new car had just arrived in the company car park, so why are we not getting the pay rise we expected?" Fair comment. It was a simple statement which could not be argued against. It was not only my car which angered the drivers, but the fact that all senior managers had a new car of their choice every three years. My Ford Estate hatchback did not go down well. It was a period of unsettling and divisive human relations within businesses, and W&P was no exception.

Carys was now in her first year of secondary school while Wendy, now a nine-year-old schoolgirl, was enjoying herself by grooming and looking after a pony called 'Sunny' at Newport. She had a weekly visit to stables to ride the pony, with the added attraction of occasional Saturdays when she competed in events at various gymkhanas in Fife. Wendy and I occasionally set off alone with me towing Sunny in a horse box. With a collection of impressive rosettes stuck to her bedroom wall, she became quite an accomplished competitor. My time-consuming efforts to get Sunny in and out of the horse box ought to have won me rosettes too, but sadly there was no event for that hazardous trick – although I did get an occasional 'kick' out of it.

Despite Harry's attempt to find improved profits, the self-drive venture was not successful. It was to be the company's only trading experiment outside food distribution. In hindsight, it could be argued that the sour fruits of the winters of discontent had hampered profit growth and was not helpful when trying to diversify. He told me that in the depressed economic climate, hiring was preferable to buying and leasing – it seemed logical in such difficult times.

Progress continued. I managed to develop training in the company linked with the Wholesale Grocers' Association, and I attended their monthly board meetings. My work with the divisional directors and my regular visits to all the company locations began to bear fruit in that disciplinary matters were dealt with promptly. On only a few occasions would an employee 'wrongly' believe they had been unfairly dismissed, resulting in a claim being made to an industrial tribunal. I found that because warnings to staff who made claims had been given, and the proper communications had been followed, I succeeded in arguing the company's case and won tribunal 'battles' – thus escaping any costly court awards and a hefty legal bill from the lawyers. An approach was made to me by the company's legal adviser (the same gentleman I had feared would not appreciate me taking away tribunal business from his city practice) to join the Dundee Chamber of Commerce's industrial relations committee, and I found this beneficial as I was kept completely up-to-date by my colleagues on the committee and the general discussions about changes in employment law. It was now immediately possible for me to chat by telephone with other Personnel Managers in the city to clarify various aspects of new legislation.

My meetings with Harry had been running smoothly, and he was pleased with the structure as he found my observations during my visits to every part of the company helpful. With perhaps the 'self-drive' venture collapse, or whatever boardroom dynamics were going on, I had a most serious shock when Harry called me on the phone to join him in his office only to receive the devastating news that he was to leave the company. My history with Harry had started in 1969 with my training needs analysis work, and he had guided me all along in my Delivered Grocery days – and, more recently, we had what I felt was an advantageous 'group' arrangement. Clearly somewhere there was a problem within the Board of which I knew nothing.

When I met him in his office, I was almost speechless and could only offer my condolences – it wasn't for me to enquire into the whys and the wherefores. My private thoughts were that the stagnant profit situation and the move into the vehicle hire market had not been helped by the country's economic malaise – collectively they had claimed a victim. I thanked Harry for all his help and encouragement, and wished him every success. I was not to meet him for another twenty years. A sad day.

That's a huge personal loss, Robbie Murray. Harry was the man who gave you a golden opportunity to progress. Soldier on!

* * *

In the Chairman's report of 1980, Mr Hadden announced the company's market capitalisation stood at over £5m with sales in excess of £70m, but with pressures coming from superstores such as Wm Low & Co. our delivered grocery division profits had been maintained only at the level for previous years of £0.5m

Following Harry's exit, Mr Hadden became Chief Executive and all the directors and myself reported to him. One of my Central Office colleagues, Murray McGregor, was promoted to the post of Company Secretary and continued to report to Mr Hadden.

An embarrassing moment occurred in November 1981. With two friends, Peter Close and Norman McLeod from St Andrews, I set off to walk in the area of Jock's Road, in the Grampians, on Sunday the 9th. We had walked together previously that year along the Fife coast on the 'Chain Walk' and in the Perthshire mountains, but had not walked as much as we planned. It was unusual to walk in November, but we thought it would be a short walk to round off the year. It was a mistake. In a matter of a few minutes, we were shrouded in very thick mist. We tried unsuccessfully to retrace our steps to Jock's Road, but ended up spending the night on a mountain. Luckily my plastic, orange-coloured survival bag, hitherto unused, kept me and my wet feet reasonably warm. It was a mild night with no frost or rain. Our absence at home triggered off a search, and at first light we had the humbling experience of being picked up by helicopter. We were back at the car park in a few minutes, and were asked a few searching questions about our kit. We were able to report we had food left, our walking gear was adequate, and we had every item with us except a torch which – in any event – would not have helped much. After a shower and tidy up at home I had even more embarrassment when I arrived at the office, unfortunately at lunchtime, and had to 'run the gauntlet' in the canteen to the numerous cheeky and humorous remarks – including Eddie's loudest observation: "Oh no, don't tell me they found him!"

My association with that Remembrance Sunday is that it was the day Michael Foot caused some disquiet when he attended the Centotaph service wearing a donkey jacket.

Regular meetings with location managers kept me fully up-to-date on trading developments. News within Catering was that Aberdeen was growing stronger with oil-related business, the main feature being that instant reactions were expected by oil companies to supply a rig or vessel while at the same time being tardy with payment agreements. Now that Raymond Green had retired, Charles Philip was the new young blood successfully holding the fort. The Edinburgh, Newhaven branch had been closed, as it was found the improving road network allowed economic deliveries from the Glasgow branch to cover the Lothians area.

One day when I visited Invergowrie branch, I popped in to see the buyers and sales people. The sales reps were out and about, but I happened to meet Mike Rae, the Marketing Manager. "How are things, Mike?" I asked him.

"Recovering from a shock," was the worrying reply.

"Oh? What's that?"

"It's a heck of a story, and you could have been involved if things had gone wrong."

I was puzzled. "So it all ended happily, then?"

"It was 50/50 for a while," he told me. "Possibly worse than that. Have you got time to listen?"

"Go on."

"Well, you know we have growth in off-shore accounts at our Aberdeen branch?"

"Sure."

"Okay. Well, the oil business is excellent, but you must be prepared to receive catering orders by teleprinter, and within hours process the order and deliver it to an oil rig company's supply vessel at the harbour. It's critical, otherwise you lose the account. We had a giant account with a company to supply two offshore self-propelled rigs in the North Sea. Evidently, a few weeks went past before our 'Offshore Contracts Manager' noticed no follow-up orders... and when he enquired with the company, he was informed the rigs were now on charter to a new operator and both rigs were in the 'Med' off the coast of Libya. With the debt over £250k, Mr Hadden told the offshore contracts manager, 'You must get to Libya and bring back the money!'

"With relations between the UK and Libya strained, the Foreign Office had to be contacted for advice – such as 'pairing' with another Brit in Libya, taking only items which may be confiscated by Libyan authorities, and to have US Dollar notes slipped inside a passport when inspected. With only one plane per week in or out of Libya, he would have to reside in a work camp for a week, He did get the money in mixed cash of several currencies, and had it secreted to get through customs. As soon as he got to London, he banked it with the RBS."

"What a gamble to get that amount of money out of Libya!" I exclaimed, amazed to hear the account.

"I'm still trembling at the thought of how Mr Hadden would have reacted to a bad debt of £250k," he confided.

"I have to say, Mike, I would not have been too pleased to go to a Libyan prison with a lawyer to try and secure his release."

"It was a daring trip to make and all was well, though it indicates just how difficult the oil business can be."

"At least you can relax now, Mike," I told him.

* * *

Although I had been aware that members of a branch of the Institute of Personnel Management met regularly in Dundee, I had not been able to attend meetings. While discussing some legal issues with a fellow personnel specialist I was invited to join the local branch. After a few monthly meetings, I found the opportunity to chat about pertinent issues very helpful. Later, I found that several 'professional institutes' also held regular meetings in the city.

One problem I discovered was that, individually, each Institute found it difficult to muster sufficient support to attract high profile after-dinner speakers. An idea put forward by the British Institute of Management branch was to combine each institute into a body called Tayside Association of Professional Institutes (TAPIS), with the sole purpose of arranging one-off high-profile meetings.

This proved to be an excellent idea, and TAPIS began to invite some 'big' names. The politician Enoch Powell was one such sought-after speaker, and TAPIS filled the Angus Hotel when he came to speak. Later Mr James Gulliver, then Chief Executive of Argyle Foods, was invited to speak. Since he was obviously a giant figure in the grocery world, I had the honour of being appointed 'Chairman' of the project. This required me to meet Mr Gulliver when he arrived at Dundee Airport in his private jet and guide him to his accommodation in the Angus Hotel in the Lord Provost's official City car 'TS1'. Any concerns I had about meeting such a high-powered man disappeared immediately when I found him to have the quiet demeanour of a kindly, soft-spoken uncle. I chaired a most enjoyable and successful evening, which was one of my business highlights.

Frank Keanie had encouraging news in that he secured the biggest Cash and Carry depot in Scotland, owned by John

Stokes. The take-over of the depot at Blochairn in Glasgow was a major step for Frank. This was one of the most impressive take-overs, as it was a major player in a prime trading site. Clearly there were indications for further acquisitions.

Import division presented me with little need to get involved. Mr Iain Philip concentrated on importing and sourcing product, while the factory – although I did visit it on an irregular basis – required no action. Meanwhile, Eddie had been doing his best to raise the profile of VG. While his youthful football-following roots lay with Motherwell Football Club (and his Rangers leaning was merely, I guessed, a religious choice), Eddie had formed a determined effort to find influence with Dundee United FC under the ownership and control of the acclaimed Jim McLean – a successful manager who was making great strides with a young team. My perception (although I may have been wrong) was while Eddie was delighted to promote and supply team shirts with the VG logo, his aspirations seemed to be for shares in the control of the club.

When Eddie wasn't present at the lunch table, there were occasional careful comments about his possible long-term ambitions. On more safe ground, the conversations were once more centred on Scotland's football abilities. Having played well and lost only one game in a difficult 'qualifiers' group of Sweden, Portugal, Israel and Northern Ireland, Scotland's coach – the highly-respected Jock Stein – did not manage to advance, having drawn with the Soviet Union, winning against New Zealand and losing heavily to Brazil. In a continuing and prolonged disruptive period politically and economically in Britain, the friendly banter in the canteen was a welcome digression.

The following three years up to 1983 had seen some tell-tale signs of the impact each division was having in its own sphere. Catering, with a more advantageous profit margin, was holding its own position within the Group. Delivered Grocery was striving to find volume. The realisation of supplying the retail customers was that retail competition by the multiples was intensifying but also, as a wholesaler, W&P had a declining impact to influence their retailer's purchases. In fact, the stark truth was that the warehouse simply delivered what the shopkeeper needed. Yet again, more volume was required.

Frank's determined efforts to raise the performance of the Cash and Carry division were paying off. He was expanding depots with the acquisition of a depot in Edinburgh and across the border in Morpeth. All of the company's attempts at growth were remarkable, while the general state of the entire UK was in disarray. The UK's 1980 unemployment figure of 2m soared to 3.2m in 1983, representing 11.5% of the working population. Some measurements at the worst moments rose to 14%. Inflation raged throughout this period between 8% to 11.8%. Little wonder some companies such as British Steel had employees on strike in search of a 20% pay rise. IRA activities added to the gloom, with 17 people killed in a Harrods blast and a parcel bomb sent to the Prime Minister, Mrs Thatcher.

I clearly recall being on a family summer holiday at a friend's house in Surrey and one day visiting Central London along with one of our hosts' children. While we were ignorant of the situation, the family's mum had heard on an afternoon TV newsflash of a bomb blast in the capital, and in the days before mobile phones she was at her wit's end waiting at her front door until we all arrived home in one piece.

The general national scene was one of chaos and destruction, with large-scale protest marches in Glasgow, London and Manchester. Closures became commonplace, with the threat of *The Times* newspaper closing unless a buyer could be found. Widespread coal-pit closures were announced, and British Leyland closed three factories. To add to the gloom the, Linwood Talbot plant at Linwood in Scotland closed its doors. Back in 1966, while on my teacher training course at Jordanhill College, I had been able to visit the Talbot plant and it seemed to have a bright future – but during the 1970s and 80s, foreign car manufacturers were invading the British market.

There seemed to be no end to the scale and the variety of troubles in those early 1980s. It seemed bizarre that other news of the time included the Queen opening a new indoor shopping centre at Telford, Enoch Powell's 'Rivers of Blood' speech warned of racially-based civil unrest, and a new law giving the right to buy council houses was passed. The M4 was opened, and wheel clamps were introduced. A typical British cocktail of events, but life went on – somehow.

An example of this was the company's acquisition in 1983 of G&P Merchants, a grocery wholesale business based in Aberdeen, which supplied Spar retailers. This once-robust business was obviously facing the same threats as Eddie's Division and succumbed to the fight with multiple supermarkets. This acquisition was, in later years, set to create quite life changing moments within W&P.

It was another one of those days when all 'hands on deck' were required to assist with the stocktake at Aberdeen. The scale of this was significant. Centra acquisitions had come along and the symbol eventually removed when the business was integrated, but this was a major symbol group wholesaler servicing a string of over 50 Spar shops in the north. Additionally, G&P Merchants operated nineteen wholly-owned retail shops operating under the name of 'Mackies Stores'. Clearly the owners had been on the right path in that they had recognised the need to control and develop their own retail stores. The fact they had run into trouble obviously indicated the strength of the tide against them – and indeed, illustrated the sweep of the currents Eddie too was fighting.

It was clear from the outset that the Spar symbol would be retained, which resulted in stocking the Spar own-brand products in the Dundee warehouse. Dennis was now in a position of operating bigger and more economic runs with larger vehicles, while Alex and his team in the Buying office were coping with sales promotions and stocking for both VG and Spar customers.

The dynamics for Eddie had changed overnight. He appointed one of his VG sales consultants to manage what were now his wholly-owned shops. My involvement came when he was forced to analyse the profit contribution and geographic location of his new shops, and concluded that some must go. In the end nine shops were closed without significant detrimental impact on profit, and redundancies resulted.

It may not have seemed at the time to be a period when W&P was repositioning the business, but that is what was happening. Delivered grocery was now in the 'wholly-owned shop' world, albeit with only ten shops. Eddie, a wholesaler at heart, was now in a position to influence his retailers by further developing his 'small multiple'. Gradually I was able to be more involved, and found myself back in a retail context – just like my earlier Willie Low's days.

Cash and Carry was expanding and so too was Catering, while a decision was taken by the Board to close the factory. With the combined effects of general countrywide work-force dissatisfaction and the multitude of new or amended employment legislation, I found myself representing the company in a growing number of unfair dismissal tribunal cases. Whatever amateur skills I possessed, I was heartened by my 'victories' and my confidence grew.

Don't get too carried away now, Murray – remember, you are a personnel manager and not a lawyer. You'll come a cropper someday – don't get too cocky!

* * *

Carys had achieved her necessary scholastic qualifications and had decided to study law. It was a proud moment as I drove her across the Tay Road Bridge one quiet late-September evening in 1983 when she set off to attend a briefing meeting at Dundee University. I was filled with admiration for her courage as I watched her stride, with seeming confidence, towards the law faculty building. That was her off on her own voyage of discovery. "Good luck, lass," I murmured as I drove off.

When I remarked to one of my colleagues, a personnel director in a jute company, on the Chamber of Commerce Industrial Relations Committee about the growing stresses of keeping up-to-date with legal requirements, he replied succinctly: "That's not a problem, Bob. Boards need us more than ever. It keeps us in business."

Mr Hadden, I'm pretty sure, probably thought my Industrial Relations activities with the Chamber were not entirely necessary, but as it happened the same senior legal adviser who also advised W&P – and who also attended the IR committee – suggested one day that I should consider taking over the chair of the committee when the present incumbent retired. To the outside world it may have appeared that, with Chamber and Grocers' Association connections, I was too involved outside the company. But my firm belief was that W&P was a beneficiary. Mr Hadden may have been forming a different view, however.

It was while I was attending the Wholesale Grocers' Association spring weekend conference in 1986, in Aviemore, that another one of those earth-shattering moments happened. It was a Friday afternoon, and I had just arrived in the Coylumbridge Hotel when my room telephone rang. It was Mr Hadden. "Could you come to my room, Bob, please?" he asked me.

"Sure," I replied.

I must confess to a sense of trepidation at the request. *What on earth is going on? What have I done? Or not done? What's gone wrong?*

"Bob, I've got some sad news," Mr Hadden told me on my arrival. "Frank Keanie's been in a car accident on the way here."

"Oh no!" I exclaimed. "How serious?"

"His car went off the road and hit a tree, then went on fire. A body was recovered. It's almost certainly Frank, but that can't be confirmed yet."

In my sheer disbelief, I recall saying something like: "We can't remain here, can we?"

"No, we can't," he responded. "Once I've spoken with our other W&P colleagues, we should return home."

To this day, I clearly recall the ensuing 48 hours when my home phone never stopped ringing and I made numerous calls to colleagues. What a tragedy, especially when things had been going so well. Frank had recently held a major Cash and

Carry launch meeting in Gleneagles Hotel, when he told the assembled group of suppliers that he was rebranding his depots. They were to become "Trademarkets". This in itself would not directly bring in extra business, but it was a PR event to tell the trade and all the trade press of his news. This had been typical of Frank's lively approach.

Over the years, he had built a structure whereby he introduced Calder Sturrock – a young, experienced accountant from Central Office who was engaged to control the budget process and financial controls for Trademarkets. Frank also introduced an improved management reporting structure, where he had two Operation Managers – Alistair Jack covering east depots, and Ian Ballantyne supervising the west locations. With great support to me on personnel and training aspects, he appointed Bill Pollock as Training Manager with whom I had regular meetings. On marketing and sales, he had Graham Bowie, who specialised in special deals, advertising and promotions. I remember that, sometime in the 1990s, Calder Sturrock told me he'd had thirteen valuable years in Central Office reporting in to senior accountants and directors prior to joining Cash and Carry where he found himself very happily engaged, as he said, 'being nearer the pit face'.

Later, when the divisions were formed into separate companies, Calder was appointed Financial Director. One of many examples in the W&P Group where an individual made a great contribution and enjoyed a long service career. Frank ensured that a structure of experienced and capable people was in position, and when he died so unexpectedly his clever planning was a saviour. His replacement was Simon Kirkpatrick, who was an experienced Cash and Carry senior manager based in England.

Sometime after Frank's death, I met Alistair when I was on my travels around depots. We chatted about how his Operations Management role was going. "It's been a great move for you, Alistair, and your East Region depots are flourishing," I remarked to him.

"I was so fortunate in getting an excellent grounding in Cash and Carry," he said. "It's been a huge help to me."

"You were around in 1969 when I joined W&P, and I'm sure I first met you when you were a management trainee. When did you start work in the company?"

"I started as a sixteen-year-old Commercial Apprentice in the office, working for Frank and J.B.T. Then I became J.B.T.'s PA for a couple of years – sounds a pretty grand title, I know, but I got a wide overview of the whole Cash and Carry operation."

"We probably should follow that route for trainees today," I remember saying to him. "I wasn't involved in Cash and Carry until 1975. Do you remember who managed which depots in those early days?"

Without any hesitation Alistair reeled off: "Dundee, George McDonald. Greenock, Isaac Parks. Kilmarnock, Bobby White. Maryhill, Graham Tannock. Paisley, Bobby McIntosh."

"Etched in your memory!" I smiled. "We should really be developing trainees as you were."

"You're right, Bob, but we seem to have grown so quickly in recent years. After two or three years as a Management trainee, I was appointed manager at Kirkcaldy."

"Yes, they were good years of preparation. And after four years you got the newly-created post of Operations Manager," I noted. "You're a good example of progression in the company, Alistair."

"Frank was a great leader," he said with sincerity. "He guided me on every step; we'll all miss him."

Another personal tragedy, Robbie. Just when things were going so well. It brings home that working life is not all about sales and profits – it's the formed relationships with colleagues that develop. Frank was a larger-than-life character who had made his mark. Soldier on!

More recently I met Graham Bowie, Frank's sales and marketing manager, who related a story to me: "A year or two before Frank died, Trademarket hosted a fantastic suppliers' presentation at Gleneagles Hotel to launch The Collection Club. An agency, based down south, helped us with all the marketing for the prestigious event, and it was done on a grand scale. One hundred and twenty suppliers attended. We had a pipe band march through the hotel, and I arranged for a bottle of our own label whisky, Old Troon, to be placed in each guest's room. The Collection Club was probably a first in the Cash and Carry industry, and was very successful. Frank did things in an impressive and grand scale, and had Trademarket buzzing. Sadly, that hit the buffers when Frank died, but I have always remembered his successful style."

* * *

Another golden family moment arrived. It was 1986, and Wendy had completed her school education. Now, like her big sister, she had to step out into the world and prepare herself for college where she was to study travel management. Like all parents at milestone moments like these, it's time to see and feel the independence surging in their young minds. "Go for it, Wendy – enjoy yourself in the travel world," I said. And she did.

Back in the world of work, by late 1986 Mr Hadden was able to report profits of £1.12m and figures revealed that Delivered Grocery, to Eddie's delight, emerged as the strongest contributor. At that AGM, Mr Hadden was able to report a new face had joined the main board: a gentleman by the name of Mr Ian Macpherson. The arrival of Mr Macpherson created a buzz around the offices. He was a high-profile figure in the world of business and finance, having been Deputy Chief Executive of the British Linen Bank, and the feeling was that something 'big' must happen someday.

In times gone by business matters had never been discussed at the lunch table, but somehow there was now an opening up of conversations about our company, its growth and what the future held. Jock Stein did a marvellous job to see Scotland's football team reach a play-off with Australia to qualify for the 1986 FIFA tournament, but at his glorious moment of triumph he suddenly collapsed and died. He was never to see his team beat Australia. This was one of our saddest chats about Scotland's World Cup adventures. Jock was a strong character, and it was possibly only his experience that may have seen Scotland succeed beyond round one. The group was one of the toughest ever faced by a Scottish squad – Denmark, West Germany and Uruguay – and once again we didn't proceed to round two.

If the acquisition of Blochairn Cash and Carry depot was physically the largest, then it was almost dwarfed by the addition of J.W. Smalley's depot at Somercotes, Derbyshire. Cash and Carry was growing rapidly. The period from 1973 to 1987 was one of steady expansion, and what is truly astonishing is that during that entire fourteen-year period whilst seeing modest company growth, albeit with 'sticky' profit expansion, the UK suffered the most disruptive, damaging and morale-sapping time since the Second World War.

Amidst the gloom, I received the wonderful news that Carys had successfully completed her Law degree studies and her administrative year. Later, on a sunny afternoon in the early summer of 1987, Carys – having successfully completed her law studies – collected her First Class degree diploma and Employment Law Gold medal at the graduation ceremony in Caird Hall, Dundee.

I look back on the 1970s as a period when great attention was being paid to management training, and I wrongly assumed that in the world of business some thoughts were paid to systems and procedures – but clearly they were not. Perhaps that reflected my entry into the world of management at a time when training boards were set up, and my fortune at being able to attend management courses in the city of Dundee. Today I look back on a few cases, especially in the 1980s, which may been avoided by better management. It's easy in hindsight, but the Piper Alpha blaze, King's Cross fire, the Zeebrugge ferry disaster and possibly the Hillsborough tragedy may never have happened if better management planning and controls had been applied. It's a well-known fact that tragedies are catalysts to rethink rules, procedures and human behaviour in the workplace.

By far the impact which is most relevant in my story about W&P is that the company and many like it had to find ways to survive and grow in the turbulent cauldron of the UK during the 1970s and 80s – when so much change was going on: political indecision, social unrest, the state of 'flux' in the post-war years taking effect, and a frustrated population seeking a quicker and better standard of living. There seemed to be so many paradoxes – football players earning £1m transfer fees and millions of new foreign motorcars being imported or made in the UK, while old traditional industries were going under. It was a time of social and economic change.

No wonder our canteen chats were so lively – there existed a rich cocktail of the humorous, tragic and frightening events around us (both good and bad), with murder and deaths in the newspapers almost every day. And for all that, my life as a manager continued comfortably with stimulating holidays every year and a new company car every third year.

CHAPTER 11

"Another Box of Lard", "The Company Doubles in Size", or "1990: Sales Turnover £428m"

BY the late 1980s, the 'period of repositioning' by the board began to bear fruit. Cash and Carry division, with its recent growth arising from the Blochairn and Smalley's (Somercotes) acquisitions, had the bright news seriously dimmed when it lost Simon Kirkpatrick due to unfortunate bad health. Fortunately David Sharratt, who had managed the recently-acquired Somercotes giant Cash and Carry depot, was an immediate successor.

The gloss had left Catering's oil-related success at Aberdeen, but Charles Philip was – as per his greatest wish – switched to co-ordinate sales and marketing activities. David Shentall had decided to leave the company to pursue another career in the hospitality sector, and was replaced by Hamish Inglis – a non-Executive Director with Scottish Equitable, who had extensive knowledge of the hotel and catering industry and notably an impressive seven-times Scottish Rugby cap in the 1950s.

Eddie's Delivered Grocery business, seeing the increased sales volumes allied with the ability to influence increased profits through ten wholly-owned Mackies shops, set about improving systems by introducing computerised ordering. This allowed customers to put through an order on a mainframe link which went directly through to the warehouse, thus reducing the time gap and labour intensity between order receipt and deliveries. The acquisition of G&P Merchants had brought with it the 'lucky' accidental acquisition of Mackies stores, rather like Thomas Watson and Joseph Philip's consignment of lard arriving in Dundee. Finding a solution of how to deal with an unexpected problem became their springboard for expanding business. Eddie found himself with a 'box of lard' – a tempting group of stores – which could be capable of multiplying. The seeds were sown for him to acquire shops and have control of both retail staff and retail operations.

With the retirement of Douglas in the Printing department and the growing need to produce more advertising and publicity material for all divisions, an economic case was made to invest in plant and equipment – thus setting up, in 1987, a separate profit-centred Printing function which would provide a wider commercial printing service including to external customers. The young, technically-qualified operators Neil McNeil and Bruce Clark, who replaced Douglas, would run from a better equipped and free-standing printing unit at Dunsinane Industrial estate in Dundee.

In 1988, Mr Hadden was proudly able to report to shareholders profits of £3.6 m – a seven-fold increase during his tenure. Turnover was now running at £225m, and market capitalisation had climbed to £12m. Coincidentally, it was the time for Jim Hadden and Iain Philip to retire after respectively serving 20 and 40 years at the highest level in the business, and Ian Scott – the recently-appointed Senior Accountant – was appointed Finance Director. These changes created two distinct repercussions – first, Ian Macpherson became Chairman and Chief Executive, and secondly, for the first time in the company's long history there was no Philip on the Board. Charles Philip, who did not seek a general management role, was the only remaining family member employed in the business.

I recall my first meeting with Mr Macpherson, which was in the presence of Mr Hadden. Ian, with extensive knowledge of London's 'square mile', was a commanding figure; he displayed an extrovert temperament with a powerful charisma. Jim Hadden, with his expert steering of the company during the trickiest of times – and who had successfully positioned the company into a promising state with latent qualities to go further – was more introvert, and yet by careful guidance had cleverly deployed his business acumen.

After that first meeting with Ian, I came away with a feeling of real promise for the company's future. He said to me later that "Watson and Philip is a sleeping giant, and now it's time to waken him up". I was filled with admiration and renewed vigour to be part of the journey that I could gauge he was on. Somehow a man like Ian Macpherson and his underlying talents provided me with huge comfort that, while the country still suffered strikes and disruption, his knowledge and skills surmounted the gloom.

Ian Macpherson was a 'driver' – hell-bent on growth and success. He did so in an impressive style. I was once in his office quite late after normal office hours when he had a conversation with a senior manager. What struck me was his incisive voice and quiet, latent power. He was obviously unhappy with the gentleman on the other end of the line – I came away realising he could have raised his voice and made some cutting remarks, but his style was power through gentle, almost whispered directions – delivered with a soft, almost invisible but effective punch.

Opportunities don't always arise solely by the actions within a company, but by events going on in the outside business world. One such occurrence was the merger between the two largest players in the UK catering supply marketplace. Led by Ian Macpherson, who was quick to react, W&P in 1990 acquired a large fast-food distribution company called Jobs Fast Foods based at Wraysbury, near Heathrow Airport. Ian Macpherson reported sales turnover for the year 1990 was £428m, with profits of over £10m.

It's all go, Robbie. The company is growing impressively. Fasten your safety belt.

* * *

My lunches in the canteen had become rare events, and in 1990 and I noticed the atmosphere had altered. With such tremendous growth of the company there was an obvious and serious 'buzz in the air', and the old unwritten rule not to discuss company affairs had evaporated – mainly, I suspected at the time, because so much about us was being published in the local and trade press. All the greater reason for a diversion during June to hear views about Scotland's progression in the World Cup. That was the year when a small country like Scotland was able to clock up its fifth consecutive World Cup involvement on the world stage of football. Having qualified, it was tough to go out on such slim margins – we lost against Costa Rica 1-0, and by the same margin against Brazil with a defeat over Sweden.

Catering division began to consolidate its position by adopting the successful practices used by the VG and Spar symbol groups. The division was renamed W&P Foodservice, and began to develop its own brand – the 'Orchard Farm' range of products. The drive was on to provide a tried and tested service across the UK, which was of particular interest to hotel, restaurant and fast-food chains who demanded a constantly reliable price and quality service. Delivered Grocery, with its original nineteen stores trimmed to ten, had meanwhile been adding stores to its portfolio and was now growing vigorously. Critically, those stores were located within the geographic areas where 200 VG and Spar shops were already serviced by the division's vehicles.

"If you are adding new stores, Eddie, ask your sales guys – as a preference – to sign up the ones where our trucks are already delivering, so long as they don't compete with a retailer we already supply," I recall Dennis saying to Eddie. A rich vein of profit was being tapped. The tactics were developing nicely.

Retailers who had successfully operated a Spar or VG store happily sold their shops to W&P after many years of carefully nurturing their business. Some owners operated more than one shop. Those retailers saw an immediate route to leave a tough and demanding working life, and had the comfort of seeing their family business continue under careful management. For Eddie, this was a heaven-sent situation that required little persuasion.

I remember visiting a shop in Deeside with one of Eddie's Store Developers (a new job title) to hear the owner say that after twenty plus years of running his business, he was now delighted to sell up and move to Spain.

"Will you not miss the hustle and bustle of your retail world?" I had enquired of him.

"Not at all!" he replied. "My very early 4am starts to take in the morning rolls and newspapers will be a thing of the past, and – what's more – my arthritis will be a thing of the past too, when I get to the Costa del Sol."

Eddie's 'box of lard' was now thirty shops: "Not bad luck if you can get it," he had told me.

* * *

Dramatically, 'the box of lard' providing Eddie with such advantage took a sour turn in October 1990. Without any advance notice or even a 'cheerio' from Eddie, he was gone. Yes, he had left the company. It somehow transpired that the dynamics between Ian Macpherson and Eddie had, under the surface, not been either workable or cordial. It was, I believe, a massive loss to the company as much as a severing of a brilliant working relationship for me. I had struck a practical and productive chord with Eddie from the day I teased him about mistakenly 'smoking his bacon'. We had forged a great, mutually-trusting relationship both in work and in social terms. I was so shocked that I drove to Eddie's home that first evening to offer him my condolences.

Yet another huge loss, Robbie. Eddie was more than a colleague; he was a personal and family friend with a long history of shared social and family events. You had a unique relationship – you trusted and respected each other, and you shared off-duty fun. Keep soldiering on!

Following Eddie's departure, two events upset me. For the two previous Christmases, Eddie had kindly invited me and family for drinks and snacks on Boxing Day. As it happened, family arrangements with my parents were already made, and I had to decline Eddie's invitation. It was also a known fact that because of the great sensitivity within the business, I – along with others – had been advised (almost warned) to avoid contact with Eddie. This was a serious blow. It seems ridiculous today that such a situation should arise, but it reflected the high drama and intrigue surrounding the battle between two strong-willed men. Unfortunately, the second event to stun me was when Eddie (equally sensitive) took my explanation about Boxing Day the wrong way and slammed his phone down on me. Our friendship was at an end. Collateral damage, and a hurtful end to what had been a brilliant relationship.

* * *

Although Watson and Philip was now on a roll, the company had felt the pressure of stagnant or dropping profits. Elsewhere, other food wholesalers were feeling the 'pinch'. The owner of one such company, based in Coventry, was Ron Jacques, who had developed and operated a business named Amalgamated Foods Ltd. which provided a wholesale service to a staggering 1,000 independent VG or Spar stores in an area stretching from the Midlands to the South Coast. Like W&P, Mr Jacques had developed thirty wholly owned shops. This was the most significant buy-out ever attempted by W&P. Sales turnover for 1991 was stated as £461.7, with profits of £11.8m. Impressive numbers, but still only a profit margin of 2.6%.

For me, it represented my biggest redundancy plan and the largest programme of interviews ever undertaken. It also highlighted a problem which had been building up for some time. Every personnel and training aspect for Delivered Grocery from 1970 and for all Divisions in recent years had been my sole responsibility, and – whilst I was able to deal with changes as they occurred – the Amalgamated Foods acquisition forced the issue. In recent years, with over 1,000 employees across the three divisions, I had been providing Mr Hadden with examples of personnel managers' scope of responsibility. For example, in various Dundee-based companies and across samples within the Institute of Personnel management, the typical scope for one personnel manager ranged from around 500 to 700 employees. I was now single-handedly faced with a workforce of nearly 1,700 people.

Events were moving so rapidly that, on one occasion, my function was required to be in two places at once. The time had come to recruit two additional personnel managers, one for Cash and Carry (now labelled W&P Trademarkets) and one for Delivered Grocery, each to report to me. Coincidentally, the personnel manager I had engaged to be responsible for the latter had to be deployed, without any induction or indeed without having stepped inside the Blackness Road offices, to hold meetings in Amalgamated Foods depots located in the South Coast of England. Fortunately Betty Wallace had a wealth of personnel experience and was able, after several telephoned 'induction briefings' by me, to deal with urgent redundancy communications. Not as per the personnel textbooks, but 'needs must'. It was all quite dramatic.

Mr Macpherson announced that W&P had effectively doubled in size overnight. By the end of the year the workforce was approaching 3,000. W&P was now undoubtedly a major UK player in food wholesaling, and a growing force in retailing.

A surprise piece of news came to me at the lunch table in 1992. Evidently Eddie had started up his own convenience retail stores company called "Morning Noon and Night", and it transpired that two of his retail store developers had recently left W&P to join him. Rumours were rife.

* * *

Mr Jacques' thirty wholly-owned stores had traded under the banner of "Alldays" and, following the acquisition of Amalgamated Foods, the shops were managed by the new Division entitled Retail Stores Management. Delivered Grocery was renamed Retail Services.

CHAPTER 12

"New Company Headquarters", "A Tarot Card Warning", or "1992: Sales Turnover £492m"

ONCE the urgency of the Amalgamated Foods acquisition was over, I had the problem of deciding where to locate the two personnel managers, myself and Nan, my secretary. By good luck, premises – in good shape, once part of a jute mill office – were found next to the city dog pound in Brown Street, fairly close to Blackness Road. I now felt I had a department which was adequately staffed and equipped to cope with the company's enhanced standing in the UK world of food distribution.

You've got a fully staffed unit now, Robbie – keep up the good service to the Divisions.

I recall with great sadness that Nan, who had been in hospital suffering from cancer and had been off work for some considerable time, was unable to join us for our office Christmas lunch at the Howff Tavern in Dundee. Nan had been my secretary for over fifteen years, and had been of great help to me. Along with the personnel managers, I fabricated a story to entice Nan to fix an invented 'problem' on a computer and then join us for lunch. We all realised this was probably her last outing, and I drove to her house and transported her to the Howff. She enjoyed so much being back in the office, even for a few moments, and meeting her colleagues. Nan died a few weeks later, and for me it was the end of an era when she had seen so many changes in the personnel office's work and contributed so much. The 'golf ball' head typewriter was well worth it, Nan!

Mr Macpherson had a similar problem, albeit on a far greater scale, in that he personally – and the company opera-tionally – did not occupy premises befitting a business of the stature of the new greatly enlarged organisation. Consequent-ly, in 1992 he secured high-profile ground space at Dundee's then-undeveloped Technology Park, and commissioned tailor-made plans to erect headquarters that reflected the company's standing within both the trade and financial world. His plan was to accommodate the 'old' Central Office, the personnel function, and the Cash and Carry division's sales, marketing and accounting functions. He also planned to accommodate the directors of each Division. From a competition set up by Ian Macpherson, the name for the new custom-built upmarket headquarters was Strathtay House. From all employee entries the prize was won by Jean Redpath, one of my Personnel Managers.

One aspect which I found most disagreeable was that the old quaint, homely feeling which existed in the days of the 1970s and 80s – when reporting structures were short, and to a family member on the Board – had gone. In place was a more 'big company' feel, and less personal identity. I think this is what I had sensed at the lunchtime chats. Some element of loyalty had slipped. In its place, employees who had no long history were apt to make unpleasant 'clever' jokes such as Strathtay House being nicknamed Shortstay House, and even W&P becoming labelled 'Wing and a Prayer'. Such sentiments were a departure from the 'old world'. Along with others, I relished the great new presence the company enjoyed, but in the air was a feeling that we may be growing too quickly.

In one fell swoop, the Blackness Road and Brown Street offices were history. My own company office history since 1969 was no more. W&P was now what the Philip family had once dreamt of – a powerful force in the food distributive world, and known across the UK corporate world.

In December 1992, the impressive new headquarters building was officially opened by the Rt. Hon. Ian Lang, Secretary of State for Scotland (later to become Baron Lang of Monkton). Mr Macpherson was able to report sales turnover for 1992 as £492m. He was flying high – by profession he was a builder of businesses, and a well-known figure in the UK financial world. His style was impressive. Extracts from his Chairman's statement for that year read: "Group sales increased by 6.5% and gross margins improved to 11.57%, reflecting enhanced buying power. Strong sales growth by W&P Foodservice (up 20%) and by wholly-owned stores with sales up 37%. Cost increases reflect opening and running costs of additional wholly-owned stores."

With a reference to the long running national recession, he wrote "The effects of the recession included an increase in shrinkage (lost stock) and bad debts of £0.5m." Under the subtitle of "Operations", his report went on to indicate the impact of the recession in the country at large: "the recession has been deeper and longer lasting than we (the Board) had feared, resulting in reduced credit worthiness, reduction in purchases in the smaller businesses we serve."

In a signal about future plans, his report included "We have resumed a selective programme of store purchasing which we intend to accelerate in the months ahead." To give an indication of the company's direction, he included "Our wholly-owned stores now contribute over 20% of total group profits. The continuing development of our convenience store chain and the more efficient management of our whole supply chain are the most important tasks for the immediate future."

It is interesting to note how the country's long running recession had a practical influence on a business such as W&P. Mr Macpherson wrote "As the recession deepened, we unfortunately encountered a decline in law and order with an upsurge in robbery including attacks on staff, ram raiding of stores and significant increases in shoplifting." Mr Macpherson had seen the potential to further develop wholly-owned stores. Ron Jacques had used a fascia label called 'Alldays', and it seemed that new stores coming on stream would use the title. The management group put in charge of this growing sector of the company was entitled 'Alldays management'.

In the same 1992 report to shareholders, he wrote "Alldays management are convinced the convenience market place is a growth long-term market which can trade profitably even in tough times. Alldays will adapt its trading position to minimise the threat of the multiple retailers. Based on the operating performance during the year, Alldays is well-placed to expand over the next twelve months. The Alldays Voluntary Multiple Club was launched in December 1992, designed to offer large independent retailers improved terms." His reference to 'Alldays management' signified how change was shaping; there was never an awareness in the Dundee offices about the title of the division, and yet somewhere in England was a body corporate dealing with wholly-owned stores. Likewise, Catering was now referred to as 'W&P Foodservice'.

The report relating to Cash and Carry (now referred to as W&P Trademarkets) indicated a sales increase of only 3%, but operating profits increased by 15%. A refurbed additional Cash and Carry depot was opened at Doncaster. The subsidiary also reported that a new information technology system was now installed called Trader-Saver, and that it would help to develop sales. Ken Knowland's W&P Foodservice division showed sales up by 21%. This has been achieved by increases in National Accounts, and by the further development of the Orchard Farm range of products. A new sales-based computer system had also been installed.

* * *

In keeping with divisional changes, Delivered Grocery Division was now labelled W&P Retail Services. Ian Macpherson had, since his appointment, been Chairman and Chief Executive. He now found the need for additional skills and knowledge within the business to elevate the company to the next stage of growth. His function was split, and the post of Group Managing Director re-created. Enter David Bremner. Regarding the appointment, Ian Macpherson detailed in his 1992 report to shareholders: "In June I was delighted to welcome our new Group Managing Director, David Bremner, who joined us from B&Q Plc. where he was a director, having previously been with J. Sainsbury Plc."

With the 'old' problem of seeking profit growth in food wholesaling (Cash and Carry and Delivered Grocery), Ian and

David concluded that wholly-owned stores would be the route to go in; in other words, to have direct influence by developing a 'critical mass' of its own retail stores. Main Board directors in 1992 were Ian Macpherson (Chairman and Chief Executive), David Bremner (Group Managing Director), Hamish Inglis and Ian Scott. Non-Executive directors were Mervyn Blakeney and Edward Cunningham.

It was Edward Cunningham who had been, two years previously, charged with the project to conduct a management audit within the Group. The very title of his task, announced at a meeting of all senior managers at the Invercarse Hotel, caused a few nervous ripples. Mr Cunningham interrogated me when he ran over his 'blueprint' for the future structure of the Group. Arising from his assessment, he had recommended each Division be managed by a subsidiary Board comprising a managing director and directors for each function such as Finance, Marketing and Sales. It was Mr Macpherson's intention to have each Divisional MD located at Strathtay House. The new titles of the divisions were also part of Mr Cunningham's vision of the future, which was now coming in to play.

One day my Personnel Manager, responsible for W&P Trademarkets, came to my office in an alarmed state. "Have you seen the paintings that Mr Macpherson has hung up in the entrance hall?" she exclaimed.

"Yes, I have," I replied calmly. "What's wrong with them?"

"They're oil paintings."

"Yes, I know. He and David Bremner select paintings every so often to hang around the office walls."

"But the entrance hall paintings are the signs of death!" she cried.

I was rather bewildered by her reaction. "What do you mean, Jean?"

"They're tarot card paintings! Especially the one with the five swords."

"I can't do anything about that, Jean," I told her.

"I understand, but they're so scary. I don't like them."

"You don't believe in all that stuff, do you?"

I had been, once a month, invited along with Murray McGregor to join Mr Macpherson and David Bremner to select new paintings on hire or loan from local artists to hang around the boardroom and office walls, and Ian had separately purchased – on behalf of the company – striking oil paintings for the entrance hall.

Group locations across the UK were now strategically based and, in many cases – because of Ian Macpherson's drive to improve – they were now "state of the art" premises. The Group had firmly become a force to be reckoned with in the food distribution world in the UK. W&P Foodservice depots were located in Coventry, Dundee, Durham, Glasgow, Inverness, Pontypool, Warrington and Wraysbury. W&P Retail Services sported depots in Aberdeen, Boston, Coventry, Dundee, Gloucester, Hastings, Isle of Wight, Kings Lynn, Portsmouth, Shoreham and Turriff. How Harry Gardner would have enjoyed seeing that growth! W&P Trademarkets, a dream which Frank Keanie would love to have seen become reality, were spread widely at Avon, Blochairn, Bridgeton, Clydebank, Doncaster, Dundee, Edinburgh, Kilmarnock, Kirkcaldy, Manchester, Morpeth, Paisley and Somercotes (Derby).

* * *

Watson and Philip had a habit of finding rich veins of business when least expected. Here again is a story of 'a box of lard'. This time, someone else's lard. The American Circle K group, in divesting itself of its ailing retail units in the UK, offered the business as a management buy-out to three of its managers – coincidentally, all named David – for the princely sum of £1, or so the story went. The industrious 'three Davids' set about making something of their box of lard and found themselves, in time, with a multi-million pound offer for the Circle K business as offered by Ian Macpherson.

That's one way to sail off into the sunset, Robbie!

On the 22nd February 1993, the deal was done and W&P acquired 200 owned and franchised stores in the south of England. This brought W&P's total of wholly owned stores to approaching 300 (200 Circle K, 30 Amalgamated, plus 30 Mackies stores), and it became the biggest specialist convenience store operation in the UK. Convenience shopping was the basis upon which VG and Spar, for example, had emerged as a force. Almost back to the family-owned corner shop, 'open all hours' model. The difference now is that W&P would have a unified marketing and control force, and cost-effective dedicated supply lines.

During 1993, Mr Macpherson became ill. He had been quite his usual self but odd things began to happen. He would turn up for a meeting in Strathtay House when in fact he should have been in London. Otherwise, he looked fine. He went absent, and we were informed he had suffered a brain tumour.

The fast flourishing retail stores business had been showing promise during the late 1980s and into the early 1990s. In contrast, the wholesaling activities were stagnating. David Bremner took the decision in October 1993 to subcontract the Spar and VG supply division (now titled W&P Retail Services) to a consortium of wholesale operators, which also supported and supplied to VG or Spar across designated areas of the UK. There had been some unsubstantiated gossip that W&P had compromised itself because Circle K was associated with a buying group called 'Nisa Today' and thus could no longer operate the VG and Spar group names, but this has never been proven. The warehouses supporting the business would close.

With Mr Macpherson absent because of his serious illness, the 1993 accounts and report were presented by Interim Chairman Mervyn Blakeney. He wrote: "Ian has been our Chairman and Chief Executive since 1988, and has transformed the company from a marginal regional role to a fully national position for its two principal divisions, swinging the emphasis behind our retail activities. It is with great regret that your Board has had to accept that Ian will be unable to return in the foreseeable future to guide your company. We are fortunate that he had provided for his succession as Chief Executive, which post he had planned to relinquish in the current year. Accordingly, David Bremner was confirmed as Chief Executive in January."

In the same 1993 Annual Report to Shareholders, David Bremner added under Convenience Stores: "During the last twelve months this business has been totally realigned. The acquisition of Circle K and the sub-contracting of our Spar and VG supply operation has turned it into a pure convenience store retailer. Alldays Management has benefited from the ex-Circle K management team based at Eastleigh, and has moved ahead impressively. Circle K has also achieved its strategic objective of becoming the 'engine' of a much larger business by applying its controls, systems and infrastructure to Alldays and new stores." He added, "Around two million customers shop with us each week. A convenience store addresses secondary shopping needs, mainly for immediate or semi-immediate consumption – over £3m is being invested in systems during 1993/94, which will see all stores equipped with EPOS (Electronic Point of Sale) and back-office systems by mid-1994. There is a robust platform in place now upon which we can aggressively expand."

The report relating to Cash and Carry included the following: "Trading profits continue to be affected by the delay in meeting the profit targets for the new Doncaster depot. This is due to particularly fierce competition in the South Yorkshire area. Our results were further depressed by the exceptionally high stock losses resulting from a number of break-ins to our premises, with a further arson attack at our Paisley depot in September 1993 completely destroying the depot."

The report went on to say" on a more positive note ,in November 1993 we replaced our Dundee depot, the oldest in Scotland and no longer able to meet today's standards, with a new purpose built depot. The new depot will enable us to fulfil our corporate objective of being the preferred wholesaler to the independent grocery, catering and allied trades in all the areas in which we operate. His report relating to Foodservice included: "This leaves us with a sales mix of around 50% in the independent sector, 30% in national accounts and 20% in Contract sales. All the experts or commentators are unanimous that 'eating out from home' will show real long- term growth." He also stated: "Foodservice will seek mainly to grow organically." Regarding Cash and Carry, he reported, "Like most of our competitors we experienced difficult trading conditions during 1993. There can be little doubt that the decline in profits is disappointing."

Although not announced, Ian Macpherson's blueprint (with the ink still wet) to house Divisional MDs at Strathtay House never happened. The 1993 accounts reported sales of £600m with profits up by 21% to over £12.5m. This extraordinary news was reported by stockbrokers S.G. Warburgs at the time, as follows: "We anticipate significant growth through 1995 and beyond from W&P. The company is now tightly-focused on genuine growth areas. Its management at all levels appears first class, with a 'systems and margins-led' philosophy that seems ideal for its areas of business. We therefore see W&P as an exciting growth story over the next three to five years and rate the shares a strong buy."

When Ian Macpherson stepped aboard the W&P stage in 1987, he probably didn't imagine a move to wholly-owned stores nor such growth in profits by 1993. Looking back, it was the nucleus of those ten stores that Eddie retained that may have kick-started Ian's thinking, and this had been seized upon when he saw Amalgamated Foods' thirty stores. But the scenario of removing both VG and Spar could certainly never have been in his crystal ball. There is no doubt his combination of sharp business acumen, knowledge around the financial world and his leadership qualities had all helped him to captain the ship on to great things. From my own point of view, I could see all those attributes and yet he always seemed to be a figure like a genial, well-meaning and 'guiding, wise uncle figure'. His untimely death in January 1994 was not only a tragic blow for W&P but a personal, sad loss of someone I greatly respected.

Tragedy again, Robbie. You have had many losses during your days in W&P. This time it's a crucial loss at a critical time in the fortunes of the company. But keep soldiering on!

It now fell to David Bremner to guide the ship. David Sharratt became MD of W&P Trademarkets Ltd. and, with Hamish Inglis now retired, Ken Knowland – with his detailed knowledge of the English market potential – became MD of W&P Foodservice Ltd. W&P Retail Services, with the deal done by David Bremner, was effectively no more. In a state of early flux was the third Subsidiary board, embracing the wholly-owned stores now titled Alldays Stores Ltd.

Foodservice had gradually built a UK-wide network of delivery centres (not branches with the autonomy of Frank Philip), mainly by a programme of new builds at Coventry, Dundee, Durham, Glasgow, Inverness, Pontypool, Warrington and Wraysbury with a strict discipline of stock range, Orchard own brands, quality temperature-controlled vehicles and a carefully-defined potential target customer profile. The Blackness Road warehouse had been closed early in 1993, and the VG and Spar wholesale supplies part of W&P had been transferred to new premises at Riverside.

Later in 1993 I had visited Ian Dutch at the new Riverside branch, which had been custom-built to replace the Blackness Road warehouse. Such was the electrifying pace of change, the new depot lost, within months, its VG and Spar business and was now a distribution depot for Alldays. "A little bit bigger than the Invergowrie branch you moved into in 1977, Ian!" I smiled.

"Yes, a little," he responded cheerfully. "Things are going really well. This is 30,000 square feet, and I now have 60 employees. We deliver with ten vehicles." Ian was proud of his achievements, and rightly so: it reflected how far Foodservice had grown.

While I was at Riverside, I decide to look into see how Mike Rae was settling into his new premises. He had joined the company in 1981, and was one of the longer service employees in Foodservice. "Nice view over the river from your posh office, Mike?" I asked him.

"If only I had time to 'stop and stare'!" he said in his usual upbeat humour.

"I remember your cramped office at Invergowrie."

"Yes, well, success doesn't come on its own. It's been a long hard slog," Mike told me. He had started as Marketing manager and moved on to National Buying manager, where he introduced the Foodservice own-brand range "Orchard Farm" and the division's national promotions.

"You then moved on to National Accounts, Mike. How is that going?"

"I started with a portfolio of medium size businesses including a few hotel groups, restaurant chains and some contract caterers," he explained.

"Am I right in thinking you also supplied the catering needs for a major UK multiple retailer?"

"Yes, one of my great joys. Only one supermarket chain, and it was over the period worth over £23m."

"What has been the secret in developing the Foodservice sales success?"

"Two things. One, I listened to Ian Macpherson's advice at a company management conference, and the other is that I have always listened carefully to customers' needs."

"What did Ian say?"

"I recall his message word for word: 'We run a simple business – we buy a box of beans and we sell a box of beans.'

Then Ian paused and looked around the audience. 'And it's you guys who make it complicated!' he'd said. He was right!"

"And what about customer needs, Mike?" I enquired.

"Firstly, we must be prepared to have the right product range, with no dead stock. At present we offer between 17,000 and 38,000 product lines – some customers want a contractual price for a given range of product, some want an off-invoice discount, some want a discount off the monthly statement, others look for extended payment terms while some want an early settlement discount. We have to be prepared to listen to their needs and adapt; that means, if necessary, getting the computer software to manage the intricacies."

"Talking about payment terms, any more stories of managers going off on flights to foreign lands to chase bad debts?"

"Thankfully no!" he laughed.

* * *

The 1993 report also referred to Cash and Carry successes. Trademarket likewise could offer a nationwide coverage with depots at Avon, Blochairn, Clydebank, Doncaster, Dundee, Edinburgh, Kilmarnock, Kirkcaldy, Manchester, Morpeth, Paisley and Somercotes. Quite a build-up of a brand created initially by Frank Keanie – how he would have relished directing a dream company like that!

The group now employed 6,000 employees. My Personnel Manager engaged to deal with Retail services was of course redundant when the VG and Spar business was hived off. My Personnel Manager covering Trademarkets was still in post, and I was involved at the centre with Foodservice while Alldays was beginning to build its own management structure in England. With David Bremner now Chief Executive, a Non-Executive Chairman was appointed and James Watson joined W&P in March 1994. Strangely, after all the intervening years a Watson was again at the head of the business.

Around June 1994, David Bremner came to my office and requested my attendance at a main board meeting in Edinburgh. "I want to examine the way forward for the personnel function, Bob," he told me. "There's a question I must put to you: Should we have a central personnel department, or should the subsidiaries (Alldays, Trademarket and Foodservice) have their own personnel function? And do you want the central role? You need to advise the Board what's best."

"Thanks for spelling it out, David," I replied. "I appreciate your interest in my future."

"No problem. Come along with some answers, please" Obviously David had given me 'lifelines', which in those days of closedowns and readjustment of the business was a luxury not everyone enjoyed.

The reality for me was either to accept redundancy as Group Personnel manager or select a subsidiary which would provide ongoing secure employment. This focused my thoughts. At 54 years of age, this was a critical moment. Do I take on a central role, work with a subsidiary or take the redundancy package? One other thought came to mind: with my employment law background and my run of over twenty successful industrial tribunals, I wondered if I should take this opportunity to study for a law degree at Dundee University. (And try to upstage my daughter Carys ? Never!)

Weighing up my options, I spoke with my friend – a lawyer of many years – and with his encouragement applied for a place in the 1993/94 academic year. My friend actively supported my application with a superb referee's statement, and to my surprise I was offered a place. This added yet another tempting option, but with great regret I would have to face at least four years of no earnings and a reduced employer's pension, and limited years of income practising law.

In the end, my decision was clear. I went to the Board meeting and argued a case for the company not to engage a Central Personnel Manager, and with Alldays retail operation in its early days and developing its own structures I opted to be based at the Foodservice's HQ at Egham near Staines, Middlesex, on my existing salary. A strong reason for this decision was that I already knew branch managers within Foodservice, and the managers I didn't know were based in the newly-developed depots in England. Additionally, Foodservice was showing signs of growth and profitability. David had offered me a tempting redundancy package and I did take some time to consider it, but the 'bird in the hand' was my ongoing pension.

With a state of limbo in my world nothing much could be done by me in Scotland, and the unoccupied offices and the number of people moving about became more obvious in Strathtay House. Ralph Thompson, the manager in charge of Administration and Facilities at Strathtay House, was set the unenviable task of eventually vacating the Blackness Road offices.

CHAPTER 13

"Off to Staines", "A Dysfunctional Depot", or "A Serious Health and Safety Issue"

NOT for the first time in my working life I was ready to move again to England, for in 1968 I had obtained a career-changing opportunity to join The Grocers' Institute, based in London. Both my work and home life during those two years based near Cambridge had been enjoyable, and I now looked forward to a new experience 'down south'.

Prior to delivering my final decision to remain in the company or not, I decided to have a chat with Foodservice Managing Director Ken Knowland in Dundee. When I was a teenager, I had thought around the idea of moving to work in London. That 'itch' had not lasted long, for I was soon on a track as a successful manager with Wm Low & Co. multiple retail grocers which allowed me to progress, but now – some thirty plus years later – I was considering the enticing possibility.

Ken's outline was positive, and the prospect of a new challenge with the same remuneration package and the continuation of my pension scheme participation was attractive. His main message was that a new depot and offices were soon to be custom-built at Thorpe Industrial Estate. On earlier occasions I had met his management team. When W&P acquired Jobs Fast Foods at Wraysbury, the senior sales and marketing managers Geoff and Del transferred with the business. Ken's two Regional General Managers were Bob Lamb, covering depots in the north of England and Scotland, and Peter Bromley, responsible for England and Wales. I had worked with Bob in Scotland, and we were also fellow trustees for the W&P Pension Scheme. Peter Bromley was a new face.

Ken kindly offered me a chance to visit the Job's depot at Wraysbury, where they continued to trade, and also his company offices situated at the railway crossing in Egham. At the company's expense, I flew to Heathrow and was met by George Mellis. George had started work as Office Manager when Ian Dutch was manager at the Invergowrie Catering branch at Dundee. Small world; George had managed the Division's first 'brown-field mining site' premises – a disused pit-head baths located near Bowburn in the Newcastle area. This was a pioneering role, and he had developed a customer base which formed the basis of the catering division's first 'new build' depot at Durham. George's success had led him to be chosen to manage the new Thorpe depot.

George was a genuine, straight-talking chap. He gave me a balanced view of work and life in Surrey and drove me around the 'leafy' parts of the county as well as the congested roads in Middlesex. He also introduced me to the area around Staines and Heathrow, along with a taste of the nearby frightening M25 motorway. "The traffic is pretty dense here, George," I said, my voice betraying my sense of trepidation. "Does it ever quieten?"

"Don't worry about that, Bob," he reassured me. "It does go quiet in the evenings and at weekends."

"It seems hectic, and I can't imagine clubs and communities exist in this frantic world."

"I know what you mean – slightly busier than Dundee, but you would get used to it. What you're seeing is the daily business traffic travelling in and out of the area," he chuckled.

After a tour of Wraysbury depot, George kindly drove me to Heathrow Airport, and before long I was back home having decided to 'go for it'. It was a risk at my age of 54, but I relished the work challenge. I knew the company and some of the people, and the 'unknown' ahead of me stirred my adventurous spirit. The next day I telephoned Ken to accept the offer and, since it was now nearing the end of November 1994, we agreed I should visit again in early December to fix up temporary accommodation which he offered to finance for a maximum of six months. "Be ready to start work in the first full week of January, Bob," Ken had told me.

With a decision firmly made, I phoned David Bremner and gave him my final decision. I thanked him for his generous options and he wished me well. David had always been helpful and courteous towards me. He moved around at great speed and had no time for small talk, but nevertheless we had mutual respect and dealt with business matters briskly and professionally.

Choices to find a new home varied: a suburb some miles away from the depot, or an area where I may eventually purchase a place. After searching the local press and a few visits, I decided upon a flat situated on the Thames towpath in Staines.

* * *

1993 had been a turbulent year for W&P. The disposal of the Delivered Grocery division, the loss of Ian Macpherson, and now my own personal world thrown into disarray and an unknown working life ahead of me. The period's brightest spot had been in August 1994 when Carys was married to Michael in the beautiful church at Inchture, near Dundee. It was a wonderful day; Wendy was a loving and attentive bridesmaid, and both of my daughters were at their happiest. Suddenly the contrast of that quaint setting in rural Perthshire against the thunderous roar of my new neighbour, the M25, emphasised the degree of change in my life.

Perhaps with that massive shift in mind, I realised my routine of walking in the Scottish mountains every third Sunday with the Dundee-based BT (British Telecom) walking group was now at an end. Determined to retain some semblance of social and recreational order in my life I decided, during my lunchtime break on my first Monday at work in Egham, to walk to the local library in search of some information about walking groups in the area. "New members welcome. Runnymede Ramblers. Walks every Sunday. Contact John." Along with a telephone number, that's what was handwritten on the postcard pinned to the notice board.

I went home that evening and phoned 'John'. "Wonderful," he said. "Meet us at the Addlestone car park at 9am. Bring a picnic sandwich if you wish." I had no idea where Addlestone was, but I discovered the roads to it on Sunday

"Give me the mountains of Scotland," I thought.

mornings were quiet. That first walk, I clearly recall, was in an area around Wisley. The ground was extremely muddy and, as I sat there watching raindrops landing in my mug of tea, I began to doubt the wisdom of walking in a low-lying flat countryside with not a hill in sight.

That dark moment was gradually erased from my memory for, as the year progressed, walks in the bluebell woods became a joy and the wonderful views from the raised slopes from the North and South Downs restored my walking pleasures. In those early weeks and months, I found those Sundays to be a crucial injection of calm amid the stresses of long days and serious work issues.

After a patient wait of several months, Ken's new tailor-made depot – consisting of a 200,000 square feet general warehouse and a 2,000 square feet frozen food store with an additional cold room – was ready for occupation. On the ground floor, depot offices were provided for the General Manager, sales, buying and admin, with a telesales area accommodating around twenty operators upstairs. Company-wide staff such as accounting, marketing, sales, personnel and purchasing were also housed upstairs, along with space for meeting rooms and board room.

Given the early days in W&P's development, when disused linen mills and disused warehouses were the rule, this was a classic 'new world' state-of-the-art building. Ian Macpherson had insisted on new builds, and Foodservice was now almost entirely set up as modern efficient enterprise. The centrally-based specialised staff consisted of a few "well-kent faces" from the Dundee past, and who occasionally dropped in for meetings. One day I met Mike Rae, the company's Marketing Manager. "Hi there, Bob!" came the voice behind me on the stairs.

"Hello, Mike!" I responded. "How are things back in Dundee?"

"Rather gloomy. The Delivered Grocery warehouse at Riverside has now gone, and we are in our new Foodservice Riverside warehouse and offices now. How are you settling in here in leafy Surrey?"

"Still in a flat, but enjoying the challenge here," I told him. "Do you visit Thorpe regularly?"

"Yes, monthly – but also on an 'as-and-when basis' when there's something special going on. Today, I'm here for a special meeting on further developing our own brand products."

Thinking of keeping my knowledge of operational aspects up to date, I asked Mike if I could have a few minutes of his time. "Sure, it's coffee time. Let's have a chat," he said.

"Thanks, Mike. Can you give me a quick run-down about own brands?"

"It's early days, Bob, but three months ago the Board agreed a list of over 400 canned or packeted products – everything from pears, peaches, potatoes and peas. We are giving them the name 'Orchard Farm', and are in the process of sourcing products with our specification. But I've had a nervous, nail-biting start."

"Oh dear. How did that happen?"

"Work became quite frenetic, and when the labels for the first two products were agreed I spent a lot of time making detailed arrangements to have them printed in Italy, then sent to the UK within 48 hours."

"That sounds like specialised work," I observed. "What are the products?"

"The products are a dehydrated white potato bulk and dehydrated white onion rings, both of which are packed in unique waterproof packaging and can be reconstituted in boiling water in the box before serving. The products are imported from California by a UK company, and I made arrangements to speed up the import by having the initial batch sent on two ship containers to Milford Haven in South Wales."

"Why the rush?" I asked him.

"They are unique products, and we want to launch our own brands as early as possible to our customers. I have a very tight timescale."

"So why did you find yourself biting your nails, Mike?"

"Everything went well until the supplier contacted me to say the ship had encountered a severe Atlantic storm, and the captain ordered the top two levels of containers be dumped overboard. It would take a further four weeks to ship out replacements."

"Sleepless nights, Mike?"

"Absolutely! I felt that I'd rather be ditched over the side than tell Ken we would have to rethink our launch programme of 'special offers' to the trade and scrap our publicity material, which we had paid for. We were about to discuss the entire plan again when the supplier phoned me to say my consignment had not been on the top two jettisoned levels after all!"

"So, you were saved?" I smiled, sensing that Mike had received a last-minute reprieve.

"All was well, the products were landed, and we are back on track. Can you imagine in the broiling waters of the Atlantic how much mashed potato and onion rings could have been washed up on the Outer Hebrides?"

"Tatties Galore!" I laughed – my reference to the classic 1950s film *Whisky Galore*.

"What's more important, Bob, is that Rangers win the Scottish Cup this year and win another league title."

By chance, I met up with Mike occasionally and he told me the Orchard Farm brand was selling well. It was regarded by the catering trade as a reliable 'winner'. He added "Just like the Gers!"

Mike couldn't miss an opportunity.

* * *

At the earliest practical opportunity, I set off on my rounds around the UK to speak with depot managers and to introduce updated company-wide recruitment, training, disciplinary and employment procedures. Total employees numbered around 600, and depots were located at Inverness, Dundee, Glasgow, Durham, Warrington, Coventry, Pontypool, Park

Royal (London) and Thorpe. The pattern of work was broadly similar to my work while based in Dundee, and without fail the occasional employment tribunal cropped up. Ken was quite impressed that I could save him legal fees when cases were taken against the company.

What staggered me was that Thorpe depot's delivery area covered an amazing and impressive geographic region. It was no accident that Ken and his team had pinpointed Thorpe as the ideal hub, the proximity of the M25 being a key element in the planning. With a fleet of some 30 trucks capable of carrying ambient, cold and frozen products, the depot supplied to caterers in all the southern English counties from Essex to Devon.

While the mainstay customer base was schools, hospitals, hotels and restaurants, a feature of the customer 'mix' was that a number of previously-unknown accounts, in my experience, were unique and reflected a growing trend in the catering world. To name a few, Ken's sales team had attracted business from Planet Hollywood, Wendy's, and Frankie and Benny's. Those organisations had determined their own precise stock range, and W&P merely allocated space in the warehouse for the product and provided a delivery service. Stock control was maintained by the client via a "just-in-time" replenishment system.

To celebrate the confirmation of signatures on an extension to a new Planet Hollywood contract, Ken arranged for his HQ sales staff and managers – including myself – to spend a couple of days at Planet Hollywood within Paris Disneyland. Ken's business was flying high; he was on his own business roller-coaster! Ian Macpherson would have been impressed.

My personnel world kept me busy – arranging courses for supervisors in all locations, night shift stints to sort out problems, and dealing with issues at the giant 200 employee depot of Thorpe where staff turnover meant an induction course was essential. By far the greatest problem was retaining lorry drivers. Journey routes for drivers were immense in that drivers had to be back in the depot each evening. Overall earnings were reasonable, but basic pay (for the purposes of, for example, obtaining a mortgage) was not hugely competitive. With early morning 6am starts on the road, a return to the depot for long-distance drivers could be as late as 7pm. I could see it was exhausting work, and a solution to the high turnover of staff was acutely required. The tachograph – a device in the cab which recorded every stop, start and rest period, whilst protecting drivers – also added to the pressures.

Aware of the high cost and the negative impact on customer service, Ken introduced a one-off exercise for all senior managers to accompany drivers to gain first-hand knowledge of a driver's day. In my own case, I travelled two routes on two separate days. Vehicles were fitted with a hydraulic tail-lift whereby cages of goods were lowered to street level and wheeled in to premises. When drivers encountered steps and stairs, boxes of goods had to be 'hand-balled' (one box at a time) and carried into premises or loaded on to a sack-barrow. I was shocked at one outer-London customer's delivery where the driver had to move boxes on to a railway station platform, climb a railway bridge, and walk down to get to a restaurant on the far side of the railway line. Exhausting at any time, but in London heat with a tight timetable I found myself not only impressed but shocked and embarrassed to witness my company's expectations. Some drivers drove trucks fitted with a padlocked metal cash box into which cash was deposited – an added chore and responsibility. Drivers clearly had genuine concerns – their own health and the effect on their family life, not to mention their legal concerns by inadvertently breaking driving laws.

After some intense internal discussions, including those with the trade union, we managed to build bonus and extra hours money into basic pay in an effort to reduce staff turnover. To this day, I have great admiration for HGV drivers of delivery trucks attempting to make deliveries in narrow streets with almost impossible access to customer premises.

Of greater concern than drivers' pay and conditions was the overall performance of the depot. Sales were excellent and climbing, but expenditure was difficult to control. It became obvious George was not getting the support from his department managers. He was a competent manager with a good history within the company, but this depot was a monster. After some close observation and assessment, I had to let Ken know that junior management were at 'loggerheads' with each other and dysfunctional. Unfortunately George was not aware of this.

On paper, the depot should have been unit cost efficient by the volumes of product being handled. After one full year, the depot was making a loss. This was worrying, and Ken was under pressure. The department heads had moved from smaller depots or, one way or another, did not have the 'big depot' experience. They were not providing the support George required, and – worse – were hiding it from him. Better department managerial skills were required. A replacement manager was urgently required for the London depot, which briefly needed help. George was invited to put that depot, which had a supportive team, on the right tracks.

A major rethink was required for Thorpe. Looking back, these were teething problems of such a huge operation. This depot produced nearly as much profit as all the other depots combined. It was imperative to correct the operation, and I had to diminish my attention to the depots around the country. Some serious action must be taken. An experienced General Manager was appointed and, with some reorganisation, the department heads were removed, deployed or made redundant. It was no surprise that Ken informed me that the situation was so serious, my undivided attention was required at Thorpe, and I had to make arrangements to have the depots attended to by some other means.

I worked closely with the new manager, Bob Rogers, who quickly got to the root of problems and after many extra hours, nightshift working and – in some cases – strict assessments and controls being implemented, we managed, after a full year of extreme effort, to reverse the depot's performance and produced a £1m profit.

After all my years of work within the company, this for me was one of those rewarding moments. It was what my function was all about – improving the business. This was high-pressure work in a high-pressure business, all within a fast-moving London area environment. My colleagues were highly-motivated people, and we worked long and hard hours. Without my escape to walk with the Runnymede Ramblers on Sundays, I may have cracked.

* * *

One morning around 8 am while I parked my car in the depot car-park I was aware of Ken walking briskly towards me.

"Oh-oh. What's coming?" I muttered to myself.

"Glad to catch you, Bob," Ken gasped as he approached. "We've had a tragedy!"

"Oh no!" I replied, acutely aware of Ken's ashen face and grim expression. "What's happened?"

"A driver's been killed in the yard. Let's walk to my office and I'll tell you all about it."

Ken was devastated. He ran through the details, and I recall the conversation to this day. "It was 6am and Ivan, a well-respected and conscientious lorry driver, had been standing at the rear of his vehicle with the steel tail-lift platform in the up position at chest level. It seems he was pre-occupied getting his frozen product on to the back of his load when a reversing lorry crushed him against the tail-lift. Seemingly, the ambulance crew said he was probably dead before he hit the ground. As you know, Bob, it's bedlam out there – there's vehicles reversing and lots of movement with forklifts moving chilled and frozen stock on at the last minute. Drivers are desperate to get on the road as early as possible. There's lorry reversing bleeps going on all around the yard; Ivan probably never heard the bleeps of the one that crushed him. I feel terrible about this. There's bound to be a Health and Safety stink."

"Yes, an enquiry. But why a stink?"

"Well, you see, it was my insistence that the drivers park their vehicles around the perimeter of the yard with cabs facing outwards."

"You must have had a reason."

"My worry was that if they reversed up to the fence, there was danger they may damage the electric charge points or the fence – or both!"

"That seems sensible," I told him.

"It was also easier for the forklift trucks to deliver frozen and chill product to be loaded on to the back of the vehicles."

This all seemed perfectly logical to me. "I don't see why you're concerned, Ken."

"You see, the Health and Safety risk assessment report stated that once lorries were loaded, they would be required to reverse into the yard and a marshal would be required to co-ordinate movements."

"I see. However, you were concerned about serious and possibly repeated damage."

"Yes, but that's only cost versus life-threatening risks."

"From what you're saying, it wasn't a vehicle reversing from a perimeter spot; it was a vehicle doing a manoeuvre inside the yard."

"That's so," he agreed, "but when the inspectorate come to view our procedures in the yard, they are almost certainly going to allocate blame against us."

"Just wait and see, Ken. There's nothing you can do now."

"Well, I need your help."

"Okay," I agreed. "How?"

"Communications."

Ken and I chatted. Ivan's sudden and tragic death was a huge shock for all the depot staff, and particularly the drivers. I mapped out appropriate letters and notices to the family, all staff, drivers, and other depots. Ken was required to report the death to the Health and Safety authority. He asked me to visit Ivan's home and be the liaison between the company and the family, and especially to keep in touch regarding funeral arrangements. Looking back, it was the bleakest moment in my working life, and it was difficult to remain professional while becoming emotional with the family and occasionally with some employees.

In due course, a court declared the death was accidental. The authorities carried out an investigation and made recommendations which included the need for a trained yard marshal, time slots for movements, and clear driving and pedestrian zones marked out in the yard. There was no prosecution against the company, as generally speaking the yard was reasonably safe and had been examined by the Health and Safety inspectorate with no changes recommended. The company signage and record keeping were sound. It was deemed to have been a 'one-off'. Ken had not been negligent.

Looking back, it may have been an accident waiting to happen, and perhaps today – almost thirty years later – the findings may have been different.

Ivan's death taught us all a lesson.

* * *

Somehow I heard the word in the September of 1995 that David Bremner had rebranded all 350 stores under the Alldays name, alongside announcing a plan to secure 100 more stores during 1996. Everything seemed fine.

It was when I returned from holiday in North Devon that I picked up word that David Bremner was no longer Chief Executive. To this day, I'm not sure of the circumstances of his departure, and all I knew for certain was that Colin Glass had been appointed in his place. Who he was or where he had come from was a mystery.

A further shock hit us at Thorpe when we learned that the company had posted a profit warning relating to Foodservice. We were all baffled; we were working hard to turn the depot around, but that was on the mend and we were back in profit. Something wild was going on.

My Sunday walks played a huge part in my wellbeing during the difficult time of the death in the yard, and when deadline pressures were at boiling point. I had the welcome distraction of visiting friends in North Devon from time to time. With the pressure beginning to ease off at Thorpe, I clocked up numerous driving hours and occasional flights to depots across the UK, but behind it all I had the buzz. The 'depot beast' of Thorpe was gradually being tamed and profit-ability sustained.

Walking experiences, particularly, were so valuable and enjoyable, and I made many friends and still keep in touch with members of the Egham-based Runnymede Ramblers by travelling from Carnoustie when possible, to fit in long week-end walks with them in England. Walking provided not only comradeship but also gave me a vast knowledge of the region's geography, local events and history, and a wonderful insight into the life and pastimes of my fellow walkers. During walk-ing chats, I discovered a feeling of how my English friends lived and thought about the world at home and abroad.

Mike and Sheila Gadd, now living in Southern Eng-land, were fellow members of Runnymede Ramblers and have read my two earlier *Grocer's Boy* books. They have kindly extracted from their logs of walks in the 1990s long week-ends at Tenterdan, Kent, Symonds Yat and Forest of Dean in Monmouthshire, and Lulworth Cove – to name a few – as well as week-long walking holidays in Majorca, the Isle of Wight, Turkey and Cyprus. After many requests from my English walking friends, I finally managed to arrange a week's holiday based in Aberfeldy, Scotland, when I was pleased to lead them up Ben Vrackie and Schiehallion!

Some of the highlights on Sunday walks I recall with great fondness; a walk to the world's first cricket ground, the inspiring Malverns where Edgar Elgar was influenced to compose Land of Hope and Glory, Hambledon cricket ground where the first rules of the sport were created in 1760, Sonning Mill on the banks of the Thames with its compact and atmospheric theatre, cemeteries by the Thames in London where Bubonic (now thought to be Pneumonic) Plague victims are buried, the signal towers linking messages relayed from the South Coast to the royals at Windsor over the centuries, and of course there seemed to be a plethora of places where either King John or Henry the Eighth had dined or slept. Rich history indeed!

Not a walking event, but an occasion I recall as uplifting as one could ever hope for, was an evening that I shared with several of the Ramblers. On New Year's Eve 1999 we enjoyed a 'Great British' concert in the majestic Royal Albert Hall followed, historically, with a walk through the closed streets of Central London to Vauxhall Bridge. There we stood and watched the firework display on that Millennium moment when some had predicted computers would 'go haywire' or grind to a halt and planes might fall from the skies.

In a recent note to me, Sheila wrote the following extract from her diary: "We enjoyed an extravaganza of history, geography and culture that was the hallmark of Runnymede Ramblers walks. What better thing in life can there be than to witness the beauties given to us by nature within the warm and engaging ambience of a group of like-minded friends? Are we walkers? Of course, we are, but we were so much more than that. We were the best balance of human friendship and spirited adventure one could ever hope to find. A microcosm of what my ideal world would be. What more could anyone want?"

Well said, Sheila! What a huge piece of my history I would never have gained had I not made that decision in 1994 to prolong my active working life and unwittingly enter in to a privileged world so described by Sheila.

CHAPTER 14

"A Profit Warning", "Foodservice is Sold... Twice", or "The End?"

LIFE in Staines continued happily, but the company profit warning issued by the Board was of great concern. Whilst I was aware of the problems of the Thorpe profit performance, I had not thought it so bad that the Board of directors back in Dundee would have made such a statement – no, something else must be going on in the background. With a hectic programme of dealing with urgent matters at depots around the country adding to the demanding attention required at Thorpe, I had little opportunity to explore any causes.

The seriousness of the depot was eventually brought directly to my door. Ken explained that I was still required to work mainly on turning around the Thorpe depot. With my remuneration and benefits still in place, and with the realisation that the earth was shaking somewhat, I saw no alternative.

You're not in a position now, Murray, to know what's going on in W&P. Concentrate on your own responsibilities... and as always, soldier on!

Short trips to North Devon provided much needed escapes to enjoy walks around the varied coastline and across the sweeping high level tracks on Exmoor. My Sunday walks with the Runnymede Ramblers continued when the cares and pressures of business were eased, and I could step in to the depot with renewed vigour each Monday morning.

John, the Transport Manager, continued to make important strides to improve efficiencies. With some clever reorganising of routes and alterations to the sections with his department, he was cutting costs. He was an experienced transport man and had summed up the weak spots in his workforce. A few personnel changes were required, and we worked closely to move out the ineffectual supervisors. It was obvious that weak management had allowed slackness and absenteeism to reach unacceptable levels. He also had a quick eye to spot drivers who could make the grade as a supervisor.

An example of John's strict way of dealing with 'slackers' remains in my mind. A certain supervisor kept taking 'sick' time off work. John had, with my help, traced back the absence level which was wholly unacceptable. One day John came rushing into my office. "Bob, I need your help – now. I need a witness."

"What's wrong John?" I asked him, surprised at the urgency of his request.

"It's that 'waste of space' that keeps taking days off. He's had someone phone in to say he's sick, and he's not turned up this morning."

John explained that he knew the culprit purportedly had a boat at Poole harbour, and he was probably working on it. "Come with me to Poole, 'cos I want to catch him. He's almost certainly there!" John, I guessed, had probably done something like this before.

"We'll wear our suits, and ask if 'Mr A.' is available to speak with."

When we arrived at the marina office, John asked the controller if 'Mr A' was available for a chat. "Yes, that's him down there," came the reply. "He's working on his boat. Do you want to walk down to talk with him?"

"No, it's okay," John assured him. "We just wondered if we would find him here."

Back in John's car, we chatted. "That should sort him out," he explained. "The controller will likely tell him, but he won't know it was us. And the marina man will be left wondering why two suited gents had suspiciously turned out to check on him!"

John interviewed 'Mr A.' the next morning and dismissed him. News of John's tough approach soon got around, and his department quickly took on a new smarter, fitter feel about it.

John had other issues, however. He suspected drivers were reporting stock missing on cages (allegedly mistakes made by order pickers), and were meeting up in laybys on roads to 'sell' or 'trade' stock with other driving friends. We toured a few roads and found nothing amiss, but word of John's tactics soon got around the workforce.

Along with the Warehouse Manager, similar stronger action was taken with warehouse employees. The result was that two key areas of big loss within the depot were tightened up. Along with Bob, we improved tea break facilities for staff, and soon the depot had an air of 'no nonsense' management.

* * *

Although I describe, modestly, my successful record of 'wins' at industrial tribunals over the years, I suffered a massive blow while at Thorpe. A supervisor in the warehouse had been dismissed, and subsequently claimed 'unfair dismissal'. I had been involved in all interviews at the time, and with statements from both a manager and a more senior Operations Manager I felt the company had acted fairly. The supervisor made a claim of unfair dismissal, and I attended the tribunal held at Croydon – acting, in my usual capacity, to present the company's case. As the case began to unravel in court, it became obvious that the accounts given earlier to me by managers were untrue and that other unreported facts had never been revealed to me. The case lasted a day, and the Chairman began to give his findings. It was a rainy day and at the exact moment the Chairman made the statement that the employee's case was upheld and therefore awarded him £10k, there was a prolonged and thunderous roll of thunder accompanied by lightning. In theatrical terms, it could not have been scripted any better.

The case served to highlight some weak and untrustworthy managers at Thorpe, and indicated how some of the problems existed at the depot. The only solace I had was that, despite the serious award against the company, I remained confident I still had a worthy credit balance arising from what I had saved the company in the past. It was my only humiliating defeat – and it hurt.

One of John's supervisors was about to get married, and he kindly invited his close colleagues to join him on an all-paid trip to Aintree to see the Grand National. He kindly included me, and I jumped at the opportunity. It turned out to be one of the worst ever wet and windy days for the event. It was held during a period when bomb scares were forcing organisers to take major security precautions, and all transport arriving at the racecourse had to park within the circuit. All passengers were then searched prior to walking to the grand-stand area. The problem then was to walk across the race-course itself. Following heavy rain, this was no easy matter. We found ourselves ankle-deep in mud where horses had ob-viously done more than simply be trained. Shoes were soaked and our trouser legs muddied, but that was nothing to the scantily-clad lady racegoers seeking a glamourous day out ac-tually losing their shoes in the mud while being buffeted by strong wind and soaked by lashing rain.

It was a grand occasion ruined by bad weather. I can't recall winning any money, but I do recall suffering a chill. It was hard luck, but now I fully understood what is meant by the 'going is soft'.

* * *

On the 30th May 1997, as I walked into the depot foyer at lunchtime, Sue – our telephonist – called out excitedly: "Mr Murray! You're a grandad!"

"Sorry, Sue?" I asked her, a little bewildered at her an-imation.

"Mr Brown left a message – you had a grand-daughter this morning, and he said mum and baby are both fine."

That was how I found out that Carys had given birth to Lucy – my first grandchild. What a marvellous day!

Amongst all the interesting and novel things going on around me, it was with some shock and concern that we were informed in October 1998 that W&P Foodservice had been acquired by the rival business Brake Brothers, which was a powerful force in the catering and foodservice within the UK. There was little or no background to this event, and it was of concern. Sure, a large business has taken us over – but why? Watson and Philip, a major food distribution company with a presence on the UK scene... taken over? Never!

All we knew was that there had been a profit warning, and sure enough the share price was falling. For several years the company had offered a share option to all employees, and share prices were of great interest. Ken's subsidiary board must have then had serious worries, but looking back there seemed to be no valid reason for a take-over because of one poor result in W&P Foodservice. I tried speaking with former colleagues in Strathtay House, Dundee, but there seemed to be no-one with any answers. In fact, there seemed to be an eerie silence.

This was an entirely unique experience for any W&P employee – no company had ever taken over any part of us. It wasn't long before Brakes' senior managers were visiting us. What was ahead? Redundancies were in everyone's thoughts. Brakes informed us that there were no plans for redundancies of any staff... but of course, the more battle-hardened of us immediately thought: "Yes, just let's wait and see."

In my own case I was visited by Brakes' personnel managers and told that life would continue for me much as before – adding that my new personnel boss (I'd never had one before) would visit me every month for a report. I would be kept up to date with events by e-mail. I'd never had any e-mails in my life until then, but suddenly e-mails by the dozen came pouring through my secretary's computer printer every day. Truth of the matter was, I was suddenly being inflicted by a new disease I termed 'E-mailania'. Dozens of e-mails kept flooding on to my desk every day. Quite frankly, most of the messages seemed to be of no direct interest or importance to me.

The 'wait and see' policy produced a mixed bag of goodies. One amazing piece of news was that I was invited, with others, to pick up my thirty year service award. It had seemed an age away when I had received my twenty-five years award from David Bremner in 1994 – a time when so much was in a state of flux. But to give Brakes their due, they stuck by their word and recognised the service of W&P employees.

For a while, life – apart from the distraction of e-mails – seemed to be bearable. Occasionally, I would be required to attend a meeting with my new personnel boss, a young thirty-something-year-old, to drive many miles to a far-flung base somewhere merely for an update meeting. Was this part of the 'softening-up' process, I wondered?

By far the most revealing sign for me of this new regime was the regular monthly meeting of the entire Brakes personnel department. These meetings were chaired by the main Board Director of Personnel, and consisted of around thirty people – all of whom were engaged somehow in the Brakes Personnel Department. The department was monumental, and was churning out reams of paper on every aspect of personnel, training, wages and pensions. There were sub-committees working on a range of topics from job descriptions, personnel specifications and procedures. It was impressive. I could see, and related to, the function... but what was it adding to the bottom line?

While life went on more or less as before, I found myself questioning this huge personnel machine working away in the background. My comfortable existence in Staines continued with walks along the Thames path and Sunday adventures. However, I was always very aware of the ways in which my role could change. Sooner or later, cost savings would be made by someone somewhere.

* * *

Mum and Dad's Diamond Wedding anniversary celebration was held in Carnoustie on the 9th December, 1999. It was a great family event with a gathering of nearly a hundred friends and family. Dad, at 86 years old, was not well that evening, but he danced his last dance with mum – also 86 – and we all cheered as they glided around the floor like the consummate ballroom dancers they had always been.

My last telephone conversation with my father was during the first hour of the new millennium while I was standing on Vauxhall Bridge in London celebrating the New Year. Despite his frail state and serious illness, he had dragged himself out of bed to speak. He had served 37 years working for LMS (London Midland and Scottish Rail), LNER (London North East Rail) and, finally, British Rail. He'd had an enjoyable retirement spent gardening, bowling and painting. Dad died at the age of 86 years on the 5th of February, 2000.

In June 2001 we witnessed a total solar eclipse, and all depot staff drifted out to witness the eerie moment when the sun disappeared and birds stopped singing for a while. This was nothing compared to the shock, anger and awe we felt a few months later when we saw images on the foyer TV screen of the World Trade Center in New York being attacked by terrorists. It's a sad reminder I will always associate with the depot when hearing that ghastly news.

Further unsettling news came later in 2001 when Brakes was acquired by a US-based venture capital equity company. "What changes can we expect now?" was the question on everyone's lips. I recall a meeting held in a hotel somewhere near Thorpe depot when management staff at Thorpe and the Central Management of Foodservice, now Brakes employees of course, were all told that "nothing would change".

It was true: nothing seemed to change, although Ken Knowland – it had been rumoured – was now redundant, or, as some said at the time, had left to seek his fortunes in a food company of his own in Wales. His level of management was now removed, and Helen Garlick – previously Finance Director – was now the Managing Director. Bob Rogers, who had done such a marvellous job to turn around the profitability of the depot, had already departed under his own steam to pursue his career on firmer ground with Bidvest – a Booker foodservice company.

Since 1998, when W&P Foodservice was acquired by Brakes, I had been in the 'Brake bubble', and consequently news of what was going on in W&P never surfaced for me. From time to time, rumours abounded – "Alldays stores were growing fast!" and then "Alldays are in trouble!" added to this uncertainty. Later there were even more wild rumours: "W&P Trademarkets have been sold," for instance. How ridiculous. Yes, I'd heard David Bremner had left the company, but why?

It was then I realised I had been so engrossed in my Thorpe world, I had not had time or made time to find out. True, my own professional survival had been in jeopardy, but I must have been engaged in thinking about my own livelihood and future employment – even concerned about where I should move to in my retirement or life after redundancy if it was to come. My sole efforts were on myself... but now, there seemed to have been strange things going on. I tried to make contact with former colleagues, but – again – there was silence from anyone I knew in Dundee. What on earth was going on?

With the inevitable redundancy looming over me since Brakes took over Foodservice, I had begun to realise I probably would not wish to continue living in Staines. As it was, my health was suffering: the bad London air with all of its pollution had begun to affect my lungs. All of these matters had occupied me so intensely, I had simply lost the place about W&P.

Amongst all the gloom, I received the wonderful news from my son-in-law, Michael, that Lucy now had a little brother when Jonathan Murray Brown was born on the 23rd of April 2002. With a birthday on St George's Day, I was delighted to hear that Carys had given him that Scottish middle name.

Over the years, I was aware that one of the signs for any manager who feels himself or herself in a 'rocky' situation is that the expected replacement company car is being delayed for some odd reason. Confirmation of why my car was 'late' came when I received a letter asking me to attend a meeting with a Brakes director. With no surprise, and admittedly some relief, I was happy to receive a generous redundancy package and to keep my car and health benefits in place for six months.

On my day of departure, I was given an emotional farewell by my colleagues. Thorpe had been a 'bumpy' ride: good, exciting days of arriving in the makeshift HQ at Egham and the ultimate move into a brand new depot – one of the biggest of its type in the industry at the time. Along the way,

I had enjoyed many successes across the company and the gargantuan challenge at Thorpe, but of far greater importance was the superb working relationships I had enjoyed with my colleagues.

With a hiking stick and compass (along with a few ribald remarks) and a few goodies gifted by staff, I said my farewells and regrettably sold my Staines bungalow. I was headed, at the age of 62, for a new life of rambling around North Devon. Unknown to me, at that time, my retirement was to create an entirely different complexion and direction in my life... but that's another story.

I remember driving to Ilfracombe on my last trip from Staines, still with the niggle in my mind of how Foodservice had come 'a cropper' and ended up as it did. And W&P too, for that matter – what on earth had gone on there? When I next visited mum in Carnoustie, I determined to catch up with my former W&P colleagues – all of whom, mysteriously, seemed to have vanished into thin air.

CHAPTER 15

"So, What Really Happened to Watson and Philip", "Ralph: Last Man Standing", or "End of Dreams"

Wᴵᵀᴴ such a dearth of information about events in the company after I left Dundee in 1994 to work in Foodservice, I felt I must fill in the missing gaps with some information that inevitably must be lurking somewhere. I needed to know the full facts. What had been going on in W&P while I was so busily engaged with my own priorities in Staines?

Years later, during a fleeting visit to see my mother in Carnoustie, I tried to make time to catch up with former colleagues to determine the events that had taken place in the company where I had worked for over a period of 33 years. Ultimately I had little success. The truth was that I was out of touch. However, I made a point to meet up with my long-lost friend, Alan – a freelance journalist who had invited me to meet him.

"I've watched the W&P story unfold and kept notes," he told me, "so let's see if I can help you piece things together."

"I'm trying to fill in the end-story about W&P, Alan," I explained. "So far, I'm on the track of W&P, at least in Dundee, up to around the end of 1994. I wonder if you can help me because, once I left Dundee, I was so engrossed with my new work in Egham I wasn't able to keep up to speed."

"Don't worry. Where do you want me to start?"

I gave him a general rundown of my move to Staines and the early days at Thorpe depot. "The start point is 1994," I said.

"Let's go back a little before 1994, Bob. In 1991, W&P acquired Amalgamated Foods, which supplied nearly 1,000 franchised retailers, while W&P supplied 200 retailers – more than doubling the size of the company – and at the same time gained around 40 wholly owned stores. Then, in 1992, the company moved to its new headquarters."

"Yes, it all seems a long time ago now. But that's all correct."

"Then, in 1993, Circle K – with its 200 shops – was acquired for £21m."

"That's right," I confirmed. "I recall visiting the Circle K HQ at Eastleigh to meet directors and collect personnel related documentation."

"It was later in 1993 that the VG and Spar wholesale operation was closed down, and the trading customers were either 'sold' or subcontracted out to other wholesale grocery companies in the UK."

"Yes, I recall colleagues saying at the time that David Bremner had sold the impossible – not assets or stock or property, but a catalogue of trading accounts."

"It was quite a clever move," Alan observed, "and that marked the move away from wholesale into retail."

"My recollection of the situation when I left Strathtay House was that shops owned by the company in 1994 amounted to around 300 – that included the 200 Circle K stores purchased in 1993, the 40 stores arising from Amalgamated Foods (AF) acquisition, and about 30 Mackies Stores – including new purchases from retailers who were selling-up."

"That sounds correct, Bob. Then David Bremner rebranded all stores as Alldays in 1995. I recall at the time Alldays was labelled the UK's first nationally-operating convenience store chain. David Bremner picked up on the name originally used by Ron Jacques in Coventry, and that's the genesis of Alldays."

"Ah, yes," I nodded.

"At the start of 1996, David Bremner was confidently stating there were around 7,000 potential convenience store sites in the UK and forecasting he would have 1,000 stores by the year 2000, giving him about 15% share of that market. I read somewhere that 100 more stores were added in 1996, but in that same year a profit warning was posted about the financial situation relating to the Foodservice Division."

"Yes," I agreed, remembering the situation. "That would have related to the poor performance at the Thorpe Depot where I was based, but I was never aware the profit situation was so dire."

"Sales growth in Alldays was not keeping pace, despite an aggressive franchise initiative," Alan clarified.

"How did David Bremner get his franchise to work?" I asked him wonderingly.

"As I said he was well aware of the potential 'convenience store' sites across the UK, and was looking for quick gains in order to build the retail store group. He implemented a scheme by creating regional development companies (RDCs). Each RDC was a self-standing company with a head-franchisee who had to put up £100k, and who was allowed to borrow capital and was backed by W&P for bank loans to develop stores. Groups of stores – typically six or so – were created. Called 'hubs', they were encouraged to grow to a maximum of around 30 or 40 stores. By the end of 1995, the chain of shops numbered 450."

"Seemed a good enough idea," I remarked.

"Yes, it was a franchise idea with a difference. Obviously aimed at the quickest possible growth. The chain was known as a "top-up" retailer; it widened its stock range with Post Office outlets, video and DVD hire, and installed lottery ticket terminals to help customer traffic into stores. That was a pretty smart way to help growth and footfall into stores."

"Did this help?"

"Yes, I'm sure it did. He was on record as saying stores made up half of the group's profit, which rose by 26% in one half-year period, and sales through convenience stores rose by 65% because of acquisitions and normal growth. So yes, things appeared to be going extremely well."

"So, that seemed alright?" I asked him.

Alan looked contemplative. "Not really. Things must have become tetchy, because sometime in 1997 David Bremner resigned and joined Sainsburys. I'm not sure how long he remained there. With James Watson as Chairman, Colin Glass – formerly with PC World – took over as MD, and began installing Alldays stores in 250 TOTAL SA filling stations and improved like-for-like sales."

"I met Colin Glass in Thorpe depot when he arrived in his stretch Rover for a Foodservice meeting," I recalled. "Did he do any good?"

"In a way. By the end of 1997 there were over 750 stores, and he reported good sales growth. 300 of the stores were run by around 30 RDCs."

I wanted to quiz Alan on the sale of Foodservice. "I know Thorpe had a profit hiccup, Alan, and the profit warning given in 1996 seemed to have been vindicated when W&P sold off the Foodservice company to Brakes for £38m. But looking back, I now wonder if it merely suited W&P to give that warning to attract potential buyers in order to help finance Alldays' development. Probably not the case; just a thought."

Alan thought about this for a moment. "The sale of Foodservice perhaps helped to finance the purchase by W&P of the retail store chain of Walter Willson's, for the group then increased to over 950 Alldays stores."

"Is that when the Watson & Philip name disappeared?" I enquired.

"Exactly. October 1998 – that's when Alldays plc was created."

"So one of the rumours I had heard was actually true?" I noted with some surprise. "Things must have been looking good at that point, Alan."

"No, quite the opposite. The losses were worsening," he told me.

This seemed astonishing. "Why on earth did that happen?"

"Simple. I read somewhere that Alldays' expansion proved too rapid and, although the company did regain some profitability, it had to try and please the shareholders by reducing its debts. A £200m rescue package had to be constructed, which meant the company had to buy out the owners of its RDCs. But by the autumn of 1999 the owners of the successful RDCs refused to sell. I'm not sure of the specifics – I think some buybacks happened, but Mr Glass had resigned."

"So big trouble was ahead?" I reflected.

"Absolutely. And it got worse. Bob."

"Oh, really? Why?"

Alan, a keen observer of W&P over the years, had been an admirer of Frank Keanie's management style many years previously and took a deep breath before continuing. "Greater tragedy struck. Nearly all the Trademarkets (the label created by Frank) in England had been sold off earlier, and in 1999 all of the remaining W&P Trademarket depots were sold to Booker."

This was remarkable. "So that was the end of that big Scottish name in food distribution?" The reality of the massive loss was getting through to me.

"Yes, after Mr Glass resigned an experienced ex-Sainsbury executive became MD. However, shares fell to a five year low because of the cost of buying back stores operated by RDCs. By 2000, pre-tax losses were £64m. To reduce the cost of borrowing and with no suitable buyer, 32 shops were sold to Costcutter in 2001."

"Did this help at all, Alan?"

"Sadly, no, and by June 2002 Alldays was put up for sale with a tax loss of £4.6 m and a rising interest bill. The Co-op Group purchased what was left of the company for £131m."

All very sobering. "So how would you sum that up the demise of a once highly-respected business?" I asked Alan.

"I'm no expert, Bob, but... wow! I can see the risks of running a wholesale grocery business when your customers are not linked to you – I mean, all VG and Spar retailers were in business to make money, but were not all trained business people, Nor was there anything permanent about their existence. Remember, net profit in wholesale grocery was around plus or minus 1%, so that is quite precarious when you have no direct control over sales."

"Harry Gardner always lived with that reality, but in his day the roots of the company were firmly planted in 'wholesale'," I agreed.

"So you see, when W&P found itself with some retail shops showing better profits, it was an attractive prospect."

"Why not develop your own customer base? Not a bad idea."

"The problem," said Alan, "was that the company was too quick to cut away the traditional VG and Spar supply lines to the newly-emerging wholly-owned stores. All it possibly needed was a more phased approach."

"The problem may have been that, as a public company, investors were looking for better growth," I reflected.

"I don't know, Bob, but W&P Foodservice seemed to be a sound company and perhaps it didn't need to be sold."

I nodded in accord. "Yes, that was going really well. Alan, I remember Ian Macpherson telling me that W&P was a 'sleeping giant'. He was right to introduce custom-built depots and upgrade standards. At a meeting, he handed over a video to each director of the divisions showing the poor presentation and standards – in one film, a mouse was caught on camera running around in the Glasgow catering depot. He introduced an awareness of standards that had been lacking.

In my day, if I'd suggested spending money to improve stand-ards of premises, I'd have been told to take a running jump."

"I hear what you say, Bob. So yes, wholly-owned stores were a good idea, but possibly developed too quickly I think. The offbeat franchise idea was unnecessary; perhaps a simple franchise model could have worked."

What he was saying made sense. "Do you think there was too much of a rush to set up Alldays, Alan?"

"I can understand trying to move away from low profit wholesale distribution, but C.J. Lang in Dundee is still run-ning its traditional food distribution business today and so too is Booker. Why did W&P not run with all of its business and slowly build up the stores concept? It had the infrastructure of supply depots to support wholly-owned stores. I think he possibly tried to run quicker than the big multiples – but I'm only guessing."

My brow furrowed as I deliberated on the situation Alan was outlining. "Why do you think David was so quick to dispose of the VG and Spar wholesale depots?"

"That's an interesting question. I'm not certain about this, but it was alleged when he took over Circle K that he may have compromised the collective buying loyalties."

"What do you mean?"

"You see, Circle K – I read somewhere – belonged to a buying consortium called 'Nisa Today', and this was in con-flict with the buying group VG and Spar belonged to."

"And so he had to step out of the Spar/VG buying group arrangements?"

"Exactly. If it's true, then that perhaps was the price to acquire more shops. Remember, there was stiff competition from the big boys like Sainsbury and Tesco who were already latching on to the convenience store market. If you look at

Aldi and Lidl, they are in a sort of hybrid small supermarket/convenience store market place. The strange thing was that Alldays also, eventually, withdrew from the Nisa Today consortium."

"So, the Spar/VG wholesale structure could have continued to service Alldays stores?" I considered aloud.

"I think so."

"I hear what you say, Alan, but the bottom line is... how did things deteriorate so quickly?"

He sighed sadly. "It's the old story. The company over-reached itself – too much, too soon. Once shareholders sniff a profit problem, the share value begins to disintegrate. By the year 2000, Alldays was forced to announce the company was up for sale, but as no buyer could be found the plan was abandoned. I think there was a former Sainsbury's board director running things then. It was a tragic situation. It was like a dying animal in its last throes, because it returned to some profitability and there was even some talk of renewing a new store design. But by then it was too late. Some stores were sold to Costcutter in attempt to cut the debt."

"I visited Dundee and, when I saw the classy Strathtay House offices at Technology Park were shut down, I realised the end had come," I said despondently.

Alan was bobbing his head in agreement. "Summing up, Bob, the aggressive growth drained resources."

Just at this point in the conversation, Ralph appeared. I had invited him to join us at some point, as he had been Central Office Administration Manager from 1984 until 1999 and had his own recollections of how events at Head Office had unfolded. I introduced my two friends to each other. "Hello, Ralph. Thanks for joining us," I said. "As you know, I went off in 1994 to 'prolong my active life' – as they say – by taking the chance as Personnel Manager for Foodservice, and I was so absorbed in the problems down there I never had a full understanding of what was going in the company. Alan has just been giving me a full picture of events."

"Yes, true – 'events' is the sad word", Ralph agreed, "and I watched them all unfold in front of my eyes."

"What were the key moments you witnessed?" I asked him.

"About the only good one was when we moved into Strathtay House in 1992 and the day Ian Lang, the Scottish Minister, came to open our spanking new Headquarters."

"It must have been dispiriting to see things shrink. And your worst moment?"

"As last man standing, I had to hand over the keys of Strathtay House to a gentleman from England I didn't know. To him it was just a bunch of keys, but to me it was the most horrific act that Herbert Philip and his family, Harry Gardner, Jim Hadden and Ian Macpherson could ever have endured in their worst nightmare."

"Yes, those big names of the past would have stirred," I had to concur.

"It was like a horror movie. Happy people who had given a working life of service to the company were in different states. Some were in tears, some scared for their future work prospects, and some extremely angry."

"How about you, Ralph? How did you cope?"

"I was kept busy up to my last day, and simply had to get on with it. What I would say is that the hard-working and loyal people of W&P continued on with dignity and in their characteristic conscientious way – those same people who had helped the company to grow."

"What is your greatest memory of those days?" I prompted.

He stopped for a moment to think. "There were so many pieces of history that kept disappearing. It was like a jigsaw picture of a brilliant company and all its parts – bits kept falling off the picture every now and then. Each piece of news was so massive and so unreal. First the VG and Spar wholesale business was sold to wholesalers around the UK, and then we heard Foodservice had been sold to Brakes. We couldn't believe Cash and Carry had been sold to Booker at the end of 1999." Ralph paused for a second, then continued: "You were a former employee of Wm Low & Co. which was acquired by Tesco in 1994, so this must have been a doubly bad period for you to see the demise of your two previous employers."

"You're right, it was a bad time for Dundee," I acceded. "But in the case of Wm Low, which was swallowed up by a predator, in a surreal twist W&P swallowed itself – how weird is that?" It was certainly something to ruminate upon. "Moving on then, Ralph, when did Central Office fold?"

"We were last – not long after Cash and Carry had gone. But we were then a skeleton with a few key people: Murray McGregor, the company secretary, and accountants Sandy Fyffe and Derek Giblin. I think by the end of 1999 everyone was gone except me. I was labelled as the last survivor of the destruction of our once-great company. A very dark day in my life."

"What about Colin Glass?" I asked him. "Did he have an office in Strathtay House?"

"Yes, but was rarely here," Ralph observed. "He resigned, didn't he, after the offices were closed?"

"What were employees in Central Office told was the cause of the collapse?" Alan wanted to know.

"We received very little information – all I ever I heard was that Alldays bosses were stocking Scottish stores with the wrong 'English'-orientated brands and sales didn't go well. But I don't think that would have sunk the entire company."

"Yes, I believe that was true, but it was more serious than that. It was a case of selling off parts of the 'old W&P' to finance acquisitions at too fast a rate."

"Good money after bad, as my mum used to say," remarked Ralph.

"By the time all the pieces were sold off, it was all too late," Alan said.

It was my turn to reflect on the past. "When you tell me it was 'too late', my thoughts immediately go back to the hard-working people I knew all those years ago in 1970. Not only the energetic Herbert Philip and his fellow directors, but the loyal and sincere people who worked away at the heart of the business. Douglas the printer, Frank the one-man garage mechanic, Bill the bacon man, Alex the buyer and a host of drivers, warehouse and office staff who toiled away doing an honest trusting job in basic, poor working conditions. Sad, very sad. So when was the actual closure, Ralph?"

"I have a clipping at home which reads that the business was put up for sale in June 2002, and later that year the Co-op Group bought Alldays plc for £131m."

"Mr Herbert Philip's dream of being a nationally-known company had come after 130 hard fought years, and then gone in almost a few months," I added ruefully.

"So how do we sum up the W&P story?" asked Ralph, glancing at us both.

"Yes, Bob," Alan urged. "You must have witnessed big changes over the years."

I tried to sum things up in one short précis: "Watson and Philip had a long slow development in the very early days, when change was slow but the foundations were strong and firm. As the grocery market grew after the Second World War, the family members took careful decisions to modernise and move with the times. With younger directors and good leadership, the company grew significantly. By the end of the 1980s changes in the corporate world took place. When I joined the company, annual financial budgets were based on what sales managers estimated sales could be achieved in the forthcoming year and the resultant profit target was calculated. But with public companies like W&P, it was the investment shareholders who started expecting percentage growth in profits year after year, and this put pressure on Boards. Suddenly it was profit forecasts, not sales forecasts, which had to grow and produce satisfactory returns on investments.

"The acquisition of G&P Merchants brought with it a 'box of lard' in the form of Mackies Stores, followed by the takeover of Amalgamated Foods bringing with it another 'box of lard' by the arrival of 30 shops. The entry into the retail world shone a light on improved control and profitability, and this was far more attractive than profits from wholesale – especially if the company did not control the retail operations. Retail was the direction to go, and another 'box of lard' – this time an intended purchase of stores in the shape of 200 Circle K shops."

Ralph couldn't resist a joke: "So, with so much lard about, no wonder things became slippery."

"How do you finalise your thoughts then, Bob?" Alan quizzed me. "Who was at fault?"

"There is no one individual," I said after some reflection. "Pressure by shareholders pushed top management to drive up profits. In W&P's case, the company which had languished in out-of-date premises suddenly had to drive up standards. The push was on to turn the business around to retail. When you analyse the situation, there is no point in trying to apportion blame to any one individual – the system was at the root of the problem. Top bosses, managers and all employees are all victims of the City's drive for profit results and improved dividends."

"There must have been a lot of interest in the press here in Dundee at that time," Alan noted.

"Not as much as you would think or should have been," Ralph responded. "There was great, silent bitterness all round. Just think: W&P employed people for decades here in Dundee. It was like the collapse of a tower – bit by bit, pieces disintegrated. Not forgetting the newly-revived printing department, which was a victim too. No one person was ever criticised – even to this day."

"What I find so strange is that from the time I left Dundee in 1994 until I was redundant in 2002, I was so busy that I did not see how things were unfolding like both of you did," I said.

"Being blunt about it, Bob, we were all delighted to save up our share options – and in the end they were worthless!" Ralph remarked with some sourness.

"I know some people cashed them in while most clung on to them. Why do you think they did that?"

"Some people had plans to buy holiday homes in Spain or France, and some I knew were ready to buy their own property. I think the reason people held on to the bitter end is that we were brought up in a successful company that was going from strength to strength – what could possibly go wrong? Our directors had looked after our interests for years. Things will come right eventually, or so we thought."

"You know, like a lot of people I lost £100k and all I can say is that it was a case of misguided loyalty."

"I always thought of W&P as a classic case study in how to grow a business, and in the end it was a case study on how to lose a business. Management students will probably get this case study for years to come."

"Yes, with the title: 'The Case of the Baby and the Bathwater'," said Alan, grimacing.

"But I have another case study to refer to," Ralph remarked.

"What's that, Ralph?"

"The case of 'Morning, Noon and Night'."

"Oh yes, Eddie's story! How did that end?" I asked him.

"Eddie sold his convenience store chain of 50 shops in 2004 to Scotmid for £31m."

"Say no more!" we all observed in unison.

Then Ralph said, "Let's go and clink a glass for the great company we knew." As we raised our glasses, I added, "...And drown our sorrows for the one we lost."

Whatever would Herbert have thought of it all?

CHAPTER 16

"David McPherson Nicol", "Catching Up on the 1990s", or "A 'Reverse' Takeover"

I**T was 2002, and my working life at Thorpe was no more. The attraction of walking on Exmoor and my newfound links with friends in the theatre and entertainment world in Ilfracombe, North Devon, were beginning to happily fill my time. However, nagging doubts about events in Dundee – when the pace of change in the company became more than hectic – still pre-occupied me.

Since I had reason to visit mum in Carnoustie, I set out to chat with former colleague David McPherson Nicol who was a key character in W&P, and one who had also experienced being acquired by Watson and Philip. He would, I hoped, be able to give me 'two sides of the W&P coin'. Luckily, he had time to chat and invited me to his home near Carnoustie.

"Thanks for giving me your time, David," I said after our greetings upon my arrival. I explained my attempts to fill in some gaps in the unfolding events of Watson and Philip in the company's latter years. "When did you join W&P?" I asked him.

"That was in 1979, when George Ritchie – the Dundee-based A&O symbol group grocery wholesaler – was taken over by W&P. I was Managing Director and the son-in-law of George Ritchie, so I came with the fittings!" David joked.

It was good to see him in good humour. "Who were the other wholesalers operating under the A&O symbol?"

"At that time, Wilson's of Stromness, Mutch at Elgin, and of course Ritchie's of Dundee were the Scottish A&O wholesalers."

"What changes did the acquisition bring to W&P?" I enquired.

"I managed to secure jobs in the company for a few warehouse and driving employees, and my secretary and one of the Ritchie family – Douglas, who was eventually appointed manager at the Centra depot at Newbridge. I joined as VG Sales Director and had Derek Findlater, VG sales manager, and Jimmy Harper, Centra Sales manager, reporting to me."

"What differences did you experience in your new job?"

"Firstly, one of scale, because VG was bigger and consequently a stronger group than A&O. W&P had a greater number of independent shops, and of course able to give retail customers better deals and more impressive promotions as well as cut prices. VG had a greater presence in the market place across the UK."

"How did things work out for you?"

"Very well," he said thoughtfully. "I had a good team working with me, and we made excellent progress in developing VG across Scotland. Following W&P's acquisition of G&P Merchants, the Spar wholesaler based at Aberdeen, we made great strides in managing the Spar franchise in the north. Similar to VG sales consultants, their development team of Retail Operations Advisers – who reported to me – opened many new accounts.

"When Eddie Thompson left in 1990, I was appointed in his place to the VG Board, which consisted of sales directors and chief executives of the various VG wholesalers in England. Meetings were held regularly in London and were chaired by Ron Jacques of Amalgamated Foods, which W&P acquired in 1991. Unfortunately, I attended only two meetings and, at the end of the second, I was informed by Mr Jacques that since W&P had acquired Amalgamated Foods (AF) – which was already represented on the Board – 'my attendance was no longer required'."

"How did you feel about that?" I asked, curious to see what his response would be.

"Being blunt about it, I felt that while W&P – a highly successful company with strong divisions – had acquired Amalgamated Foods, what in effect was happening was what I call a 'reverse takeover'."

"What do you mean by that, David?"

"W&P was the company that purchased AF... but in reality, AF management was beginning to take control of a part of W&P."

"What form did that take?"

"In addition to controlling VG in Scotland – my redundancy!" he noted.

"Yes, of course. I remember."

David went on to describe his shock when, several weeks after his last VG Board meeting, the AF Sales Director from Coventry arrived in his office and told him he was redundant, as his level of management in the 'new' organisation was no longer required. He also recalled how saddened and surprised he felt at the time. "AF totally overwhelmed Delivered Grocery division, and – with a void after Eddie left – control by AF was inevitable."

My chat with David had answered some questions I'd had relating to events after Eddie's departure. What I picked up from him was that a major shift of power had taken place and that the delivered grocery management team at W&P were, although efficient, still 'out-gunned' by the swell of big names within AF.

His recollections prompted another memory of my own. Another redundancy victim at that time was John Drummond, the Delivered Grocery Marketing Manager and a close colleague of Eddie. I still recall a discussion I had with him, prior to him knowing his fate. He'd passed over to me a bottle of whisky, which he had received as a sample from a sales representative, and said: "We are witnessing the end of an era, Bob. Have a drink on me. Things are changing fast."

David looked wistful. "Yes, a very upsetting time, and the 'hurricanes of change' had hit Dundee's famous grocery wholesaler."

"Think of the good times, David," I urged him. "How is Andy doing these days?" I was referring to David's son Andy, a Scottish rugby internationalist.

"There's a coincidence," he smiled. "1991 was the year Andy got his first cap for Scotland!"

"But when he captained Scotland at Murrayfield in 2000 to beat England 19-13 and denied them the Grand Slam, that must have been an even happier time for you!"

"Brilliant!" David laughed. "What a game in the mud!"

On that more cheerful note, I thanked David for his hospitality and left. He had – as I had hoped – provided a sense of the changes that began to 'shake' W&P's foundations.

Incidentally, Andy Nicol went on to win 23 caps for his country and featured in British Lions games.

CHAPTER 17

"Iain Roberts", "Delivered Grocery Makes a Move", or "The Wind of Change"

BY good fortune, earlier this year (2021) I met up with long-service employee Iain Roberts. I hadn't had an opportunity to speak with him since a W&P reunion in 2015, and he kindly agreed to help me with some background information.

My chat in 2002 with David Nicol had given me a feel for how the AF acquisition had impacted on a senior manager and the 'shift' of power as it related to W&P's VG and marketing management, but he was redundant in 1991. Company annual accounts for 1992 and 1993, kindly lent to me by Murray McGregor, had given some valuable insight into the top-level thinking of Ian Macpherson and David Bremner, and Iain was able to add 'flesh' to the story after 1991.

It was an excellent opportunity for me to hear from Iain something about the practicalities of the closure of Delivered Grocery's Blackness Road warehouse and the consequent move to new premises.

Iain had been recruited by me in 1974 and started work as an order-picker. He related to me that I had evidently asked him, then, if the job he was being interviewed for was intended to be his "long term job" or if it was merely a "stop gap". Iain was a well-qualified and smartly-dressed young man, and looking back I can only think the reason for me asking such a bold question was that it was a period of economic and industrial chaos with three-day working weeks for some. Iain was looking for work that would provide him with a full working week. It transpired to be a fortuitous move, as he went on to become Transport Supervisor, then Transport Admin Manager and eventually Chill/Frozen Food Manager.

Having greeted each other for the first time in several years, I asked him about his experiences in the life of the company. "Give me your impressions please, Iain, of the Blackness Road setup when you joined, and what your duties were from the start."

"I was one of fifteen order pickers," he told me, "and our supervisor was Lou Cathro. We started work at 8am until 4.30pm, Monday to Friday. We made use of the Acrow electric moving cart system and, using the PLOF, picked stock off the lower levels of the racking on to a unitainer. The cart system was abandoned, as it caused collisions with racking; this resulted in serious injuries, and was considered dangerous.

"There were four forklift truck drivers, whose job it was to keep the racks filled with product. If there was no stock to pick, we wrote the 'out of stock' item on the back page of the PLOF to be picked later when the stock was brought down from 'bulk' and made available. As a priority, we picked orders for customers who were based furthest away to allow the drivers to get away by the latest at 6am. When we had filled a unitainer, we were instructed to line them up at the loading bay."

"What were your duties when you took over the Transport chargehand and supervisory duties?"

"My hours were from 4.45am to 4.30 pm, Monday to Thursday (and Friday, when I finished at 10 am). Once lorries were loaded in the evening, they were parked in various suit-able secure spaces within the premises until early morning. One of my duties at 4.30am was to ensure that cigarettes and spirits – which had been held in a security cage overnight – were loaded. I had to make sure the lorries were parked at predetermined places, and inform the drivers where to find their vehicle.

"My main job in the later part of the day was to make sure that all the cages for each customer were correctly lined up at each of the eight loading bays, ready for loading on to the correct empty lorries when they returned in the after-noon. When lorry drivers emptied cages at a shop, they dis-sembled them and brought them back folded flat, and I had to re-assemble them ready for the next day's picking."

"It sounds pretty hard work, Iain," I observed. "Did you have any problems?"

"Generally, the warehouse and driving teams were all excellent guys who did a great job in primitive and unsafe conditions, but there was a lot of humour," he told me.

"That sounds quite serious," I said, picking up on his comments about the working environment. "What were the problems?"

"The warehouse was not really fit for purpose. The roof leaked and, when it rained, water rushed down broken drain pipes attached to the steel supports for the roof and spilled over the floor. We also had condensation problems in certain weather conditions; the floor became wet and sticky, and was unsafe. The main doors of the warehouse had to be kept open on some days in an attempt to dry the floor.

"Because the warehouse was previously a foundry, the glass roof had – I believe, during the Second World War – been tarred over (presumably, as part of the air-raid blackout rules). During hot summer days, the tar melted and caused the putty or sealant in the glass frames to peel away and allow even more water to leak. We regularly went on the roof to fix the leaks, but it was a never-ending task – and what's more, we were occasionally attacked by gulls nesting up there. The only canteen for the staff was a grotty cellar (we called it the dungeon) under the warehouse floor; it was cramped and dreary. In addition to all of that, we had regular injuries of employees because of the worn equipment that was used around the warehouse."

"Sounds grim," I couldn't help but observe. "But the humour, Iain – what about the humour that kept you all going?" I teased him.

"In a word: characters. There were many laughs," he said with a grin.

"Sounds as if you needed them around."

"We had Raymond, who typically wore his Parka jacket (as provided to drivers), and on one cold, dark winter morning he drove in to work on his moped. However, he forgot to wear his legally-required crash helmet, and so to get home in daylight and avoid being stopped by police he spent time shaping a cardboard box to appear like a helmet under his hood. We laughed forever about Raymond, and he got the nickname "Boxhead".

"We also had great laughs about the bacon department guys. Jimmy was a great 'blether', and he would come out into the warehouse for a quick fag. He was such a chatterer, he would speak too long and Sandy, his supervisor, would appear and chase Jimmy back into work. But the humour was that Sandy himself was a smoker, and when he appeared he always had a lit, burning cigarette stuck behind his ear. Smoke would curl up from his cigarette, and his hair and scalp were permanently singed with nicotine and scorch marks."

(When Iain told me this, I had an immediate picture of Eddie dictating his letter to a retailer about finding a ciggy end in his bacon – now we know what happened!) I was never aware of any smoking in the department; Sandy and 'the lads' must have hidden the ciggies when I visited.

"Characters indeed, Iain. What about the two robbers who climbed on to the Cash and Carry roof?" I had been aware of the tragedy; one of the would-be thieves had fallen through the roof. The other ran away, only to hear that his accomplice had died 'at the scene'.

"We were all disturbed by that death, because we had to walk over our roof and the drop was four times higher. But we had another event which scared us all," added Iain. "A near-death incident when one of our drivers was lying under his lorry trying to fix something when another driver – who, in the poorly-lit garage area, during a very early winter morning – accidentally reversed his vehicle on his way to refuel and drove over the legs of his colleague."

"I recall hearing something about the Cash and Carry incident, but I was never aware of the two broken legs," I told Iain. "I don't know where I was at the time, or why I never heard of it."

Iain's account of the poor state of the Blackness Road warehouse epitomised the warehouse policy across every division of the company. It was quite obvious that there was no attempt, for obvious reasons, to spend money on new premises – that would incur costly payback costs. The determining factor was the low net profit returns. The line between survival and closure was very fine. Health and Safety was not so high on the agenda in those 1970s years, but it's no surprise – having heard Iain's accounts – that it was most definitely required. "Moving on to later years, Iain, how did the acquisition of Amalgamated Foods affect you?" I asked him.

"Yes, that was 1991, wasn't it?" He seemed contemplative. "Nothing really changed for us in the warehouse, but we definitely had the feeling the company was really making huge waves. It was looking very rosy when, later in 1991, we heard that a new company headquarters building was being planned and a new Delivered Grocery warehouse was to be built at Riverside."

"When did Blackness close?"

"The new Riverside Distribution Centre was ready by early in 1993. In January and February, we had started to move stock from Blackness to Riverside. During that time, Jimmy Simpson – the VG Buyer – would send me lists of stock he required, which we would send to him. By March, the Blackness depot was closed and all VG and Spar business, plus the transferred Turriff business, was operating from the new distribution centre at Riverside. I supervised the closure; I was the 'last man standing' at Blackness warehouse. It was a very spooky feeling to look around all my familiar places and think of all the hard work and the many people I'd known during my happy and tragic times there."

"So Riverside was up and running early in 1993, then?"

"Yes, that's right. And around September, the Inver-gowrie Foodservice depot was closed, and business transferred to purpose-built premises – a completely self-contained unit, but under one roof along with us at Riverside."

"Things were going well, then."

"After the long, hard slog of working for years in the dilapidated premises at Blackness Road, it was a dream to work in a custom-built facility... but then we had bombshell news."

"What was that?" I enquired with genuine curiosity.

"In October 1993, Spar and VG supply business was subcontracted to a consortium of four wholesalers and, in an instant – despite the fact the new Riverside depot, designed to supply the wholesale business, was now up and running – all wholesale trade was transferred to other wholesalers in England and our Spar and VG accounts went to Lang's, the wholesaler in Dundee."

I had read that David Bremner announced in the 1993 annual company report that Riverside, Dundee and Eastleigh Depots would become the two distribution depots for all re-tail shops. I asked Iain, "Were you left with any business at all?"

"Yes, our wholly-owned Mackies stores were renamed Alldays, and we started supplying Alldays stores with ambi-ent, chill and frozen stock. But, with the loss of VG and Spar accounts, our 'units handled' dropped from around 23k per day to 10k per day. Of course, we also took on the distribution of chill and frozen product when the new Aberdeen Depot, built in 1991, was closed in 1993."

"So the new depot at Aberdeen was closed?"

"Yes, decisions seemed to be made rapidly."

"But there were only around 20 Mackies shops in Scotland. Was that viable?"

"Yes," he replied, "because Mackies stores were now re branded Alldays, and every Alldays shop as far south as South Wales and Hull were serviced from us at Riverside."

"That was a very long drive to deliver to shops!"

"I'll say it was. We had to 'double-man' the lorries to comply with legalities, and had drivers stay overnight so we could use empty lorries to bring stock from the suppliers Connels and McClellands to Riverside."

This was a fascinating insight into how operations had developed at the time. "So what parts of the business were accommodated at Riverside?"

"Retail Services supplying Alldays shops, the Dundee Foodservice depot and its offices, and Foodservice's central office – and, of course, a canteen servicing all those parts."

"When did your job end?" I enquired.

"In 2003, when we transferred all of the remaining stock to the Co-op at Cumbernauld."

Once again, the reflection of the end of an era. "What were you aware of during the years leading up to 2003?"

"We just kept hearing about Alldays, the sale of Foodservice to Brakes, and the sale of Cash and Carry to Booker."

Clearly Iain had excellent recollection of the practical implications at Dundee. He had filled the many gaps I had of the Dundee situation. It still seems strange to me – even now, after all those years – that so much was going on in Dundee, and I'm left thinking that I must have been dealing with so many other issues elsewhere at the same time.

CHAPTER 18

"W&P Trademarkets", "How to Fight the 'Big' Names", or "An Insight with Graham Bowie"

ONE of the most significant fights for survival within the grocery world is that of the independent retailer. This has been evident throughout my story. As part of my research, I came across a 1996 copy of a convenience grocery magazine which contains an article about Watson and Philip employee Graham Bowie. A news item in the magazine related to Graham's promotion to Sales Director in W&P Trademarkets. The report mentioned that he had joined the company as a trainee manager in 1978 and went on to work in the Marketing and Trading departments prior to becoming Sales Development Manager in 1987. Trademarkets was sold to Booker in 1999 and, because I had left Dundee to work with Foodservice in 1994, I had never had the opportunity to know about Trademarket's progress nor about its demise.

Graham's rise within the cash and carry sector seemed quite interesting, and I set out to find him in order to obtain a closer picture of his work and the development within that division. After some detective work, I tracked Graham down and had a long chat about him and his work.

"Great to see you, Graham," I said upon my arrival, "and thanks for taking time to chat with me. I'd like to know how you developed sales in Trademarkets."

"Good to see you, Bob," he said in reply, "and I hope I can help you somehow."

"I read you were appointed Sales Director in 1996. What were your main responsibilities?"

"Simply, to devise and implement a promotional strategy aimed at increasing both Trademarket's market share and net profit."

"Quite a tall order," I commented.

"Yes, but my earlier work in the division was all about developing sales across all sectors of the business and working with key customers, buying own label and non-foods, and managing our promotional activity. It was not really anything new."

"What problems, if any did you face?"

"In a word, 'competition'. You have to remember that cash and carry customers are independent grocery shops, caterers, and pubs and clubs. When you add it all up, it's a big collective market."

"What was the competition?" I asked him.

"In the retail grocery world, multiples like Wm Low, Gateway, Safeway. Presto, Templetons, and the symbol groups like Spar, Mace and VG – and of course, other cash and carry operators like Bestway, Batley's and Booker. Mind you, bear in mind that both VG and Spar wholesalers charged their customers a membership fee."

"Did that help you?"

"I could provide a free fascia and do free deliveries of goods from the nearest Trademarket depot. VG didn't charge for a fascia board, but they did charge the retailer a percentage applied to their invoice. The more they bought, the lower the percentage charge. Spar charges were quite hefty; grocery delivery cost £40 per week, plus £13 per week for a frozen food delivery and a further £8 per delivery for chill and deli. Keep in mind that Spar's cost price was sometimes greater than the Trademarket cost price. Those charges are probably all altered nowadays."

"How did you try to compete?"

"Firstly, there are many truly independent retailers running a good business who want their own name above the shop and to also get the benefits of being in a group. So my aim was to create for these traders a support package which would give them strength. Just like VG or Spar wholesalers, I wanted to provide a help package."

This sounded like a very sensible strategy. "What did that package offer?"

"By developing a closer relationship with shopkeepers and having my Cash and Carry sales development reps backed up by a merchandising team to redesign a shop layout. They would also advise on refits, better shelving, stock range, and more information on best profit lines to help them buy more wisely. Then I started a 'Trademarket Plus' concept."

"That sounds like an interesting idea. How did that work?"

"Firstly, it was by invitation only to the traders, who have indicated by their attitude they will follow our disciplines on the correct use of promotional materials such as window bills, hand bills to customers in store displays, prices and ticketing. Nearly 200 shop-keepers took up the invitation. Clever retailers found they were able to meet competition by taking up the total package on offer."

"What were the biggest obstacles you faced?" I enquired.

"The independent retailers needed to realise they must emulate as much as possible the multiples, co-ops and the symbol grocers' professional approach," Graham explained.

"What did they need to be aware of?"

"Everything from the shop exterior, in-store lighting, having a spotlessly clean and tidy interior and attractive displays, clear pricing, and no litter lying around. In short, to avoid looking amateurish with scrappy, badly written ticketing. They need to spend more time and money on projecting an attractive image. We had to encourage them to look at their shop through the eyes of the customer. They must try to be a helpful, neighbourly, community-spirited part of the locality."

"I imagine you had to try to get the best deals for yourself as well," I observed.

"Exactly. I had to think about the best ways of developing customer loyalty both at Cash and Carry level and for the retailer. One way of doing that is to do what the big boys do, and that is to have a strong 'own brand' label. At one point I had to leave one national buying group called 'Landmark' and move to another called 'Nisa Today'. It wasn't difficult to find a better supplier; in fact, Nisa Today – in its attempts to increase its buying strength through Long Term Buying Agreements (LTAs) – came to me seeking a deal."

This sounded like an interesting development. "Why was that?"

"I had to have regular stock supplies, a strong own brand label but – more than that – a shop fascia that was instantly recognised and which provided the customer with reliability of product quality and fair and stable prices. So I moved to a buying group which provided all that."

"I see," I nodded. "And did that work?"

"Nisa Today was a strong buying group, with a central distribution system which delivered to our depots. I was then able to arrange van deliveries to customers. They also used a dedicated company to survey, measure up and erect fascia boards providing an excellent fascia design and colour scheme labelled 'Day Today'. Over 110 retailers signed up to the group, which provided the striking fascia, internal upgrade of shop layout, a better range of own-label products and excellent promotions."

"You were becoming quite close to competing with VG symbol retailers. Did you ever get any comments about stealing from that customer base?"

"By the time I had Nisa Today up and running, VG was no longer a threat when W&P sold off the Spar and VG business," he told me. "Obviously there are locations where any smaller retailer could not compete with a giant multiple, but there is always scope for an independent to operate with no other competition. When I switched to the 'Day Today' logo, six of my customers were short-listed in the 1997 Scottish Grocer Awards, and another store won the 'Village Store of the Year' Award. It was an exciting time for me, as well as for my customers."

"Is there any one aspect that helped shopkeepers trade more efficiently?"

"Yes, you won't be surprised if I say computers were instrumental in assisting," he revealed.

"In what way?"

"Every small independent retailer couldn't afford it, but those who invested in scanning at the checkout or till found an invaluable aid."

"How did that help?"

"Easy; they could keep a record of buying and selling prices of every item, and saw at a glance which products made the most profit. It also told them which lines sold best. That way, they could cut out having slow or dead stock lying on their shelves. Not only that, but it told them what and when it was time to re-order."

"As you said earlier, you served the licensed trade and caterers," I remarked. "Did you manage to apply the same principles in those sectors?

"Steady on, Bob! my hands were well and truly filled with doing what I did in the grocery world, but I did – with better buying and promotions – see above-average increases in sales in both types of businesses. One example of that was when I introduced W&P Foodservice's own brand label Orchard Farm on to my stock range for caterers. At the end of the day it's all about reliable stock ranges and keen prices, allowing the trader to achieve the best possible profit."

"Were you able to sell W&P bacon products to your customers?"

"Yes, but only to the local Dundee depot."

"How about W&P's printing works? Did you get any benefits from that department?"

"Oh yes, quite a lot. Especially when the department moved to custom-built premises at Dunsinane Avenue in Dundee. I required 30,000 promotion brochures every three weeks, plus various promotional leaflets and posters. So I was the biggest customer."

"I also read that you had managed a 55,000 square foot cash and carry depot; was that before or after your promotion to Sales Director?"

"Firstly, I was appointed Sales Director covering all those aspects relating to Nisa Today, and I ran that from the Dundee office. But when a problem cropped up at the depot at Blochairn in Glasgow, I had to base myself there to oversee the depot while I continued to run the Sales operation."

Quite a responsibility. "Thanks, Graham. That has helped to fill in a few gaps I've had about events after I left Dundee. Any final thoughts?"

"Only to say that I first set out to aim for those higher standards by developing a great team of sales development people. I think that's the secret in anything – get the enthusiasm and motivation right. But there's more than that."

It was interesting to hear his views. "Okay, go on."

"I've talked about retailers, but we as wholesalers were also learning."

"Ah, in what way?"

"Simple; when I joined W&P Trademarkets, our depots were old warehouses or even ancient linen mills and the like. In the early days it allowed for good financial returns on little investment, but it was not inspiring for the customer. When we started investing in custom-built premises, we really could attract and impress our customers."

"Yes, Mr Macpherson was quite rightly keen to improve both efficiencies and image," I recalled. "I'd like to hear how those changes were implemented within Trademarkets in the early 1990s."

"When the Blackness Road warehouse and offices were closed, Delivered Grocery moved to Riverside along with Cash and Carry's central administration, and when Strathtay House was completed we all moved in to occupy the entire ground floor area."

"When did your employment end with Trademarket?"

"In 1999," he told me, "when we were sold to Booker."

"What do you recall of that move?" I prompted him.

"I'd rather not talk about it," he said with some underlying bitterness, "except to say I was on the cusp of further developing a mutually beneficial relationship with my customers. Needless to say, I felt robbed."

"Thanks for talking with me, Graham," I told him. "It's been a fascinating insight into your successes."

"I've enjoyed going back down memory lane with you. As I drive around the country, I still see retail businesses that I had a hand in helping to develop. It's a nice reminder to myself of the good times, when I think I made a difference."

CHAPTER 19

"A Modern Independent Grocer",
or "John and Doreen's Adventure"

TO set up one's own grocer's shop has, for centuries, been the reality for many. This book about Watson and Philip reflects the wholesale grocery trade sectors of warehousing, cash and carry, catering, and an insight into the operation of modern supermarkets. It would not be complete without obtaining a glimpse into the world of an independent retail grocer.

John McGowan, by some miracle, had heard about my earlier book *The Grocer's Boy Rides Again: Another Slice of his Life in 1960s Scotland and Beyond* and, reading of the professional parallels he and I had, contacted Extremis Publishing with a view to chatting with me about our respective grocery experiences.

On a warm, sunny day in August 2021, with the pandemic lockdown restrictions relaxed, John and I sat outdoors in Cupar, Fife, to have a chat over coffee and cake and after our conversation I was prompted to write the following:

The earliest independent grocers have been around since traders who dealt in bulk products such as teas, coffees, sugar and spices began offering their wares as long ago as the 14th century. By dealing in bulk, they were described as 'grossiers' – the French word for 'wholesalers' – and the terms 'grosser' and grocer thus came into use.

By the 18th century, small general stores selling food and non-food items became more prevalent in towns and villages, and were at the heart of communities. Grocers were proud, upstanding and well-respected characters in the area, especially when they began to offer goods on credit. The credit facility is rarely offered nowadays, but the grocery store – whether the large supermarkets or small convenience stores – are an essential part of modern life in communities.

The motivation for anyone to start up his or her own grocery store remains a feature, and today we see independent grocers trading under a 'symbol group' name such as Spar or Costcutter. In times past, training and education schemes offered by The Grocers' Institute existed across the country to help add 'theory' to the small grocers' 'practice', but these days – while giant companies such as Tesco, Sainsbury and Asda run training courses throughout their businesses – the 'small' trader usually has little or no formal trade training background unless they 'set out on their own' with some supermarket experience.

One couple who took a seismic leap into running their own grocery shop is John McGowan and his wife Doreen. John is a Fife man whom, it could readily be said, has 'the grocery trade' in his blood. This 'injection' started when he was an apprentice grocer with Central and East Fife Co-op, having first got a sniff of the trade as a message delivery boy.

"Hi John," I said by way of greeting. "It's good to meet you, and thanks for sending on some notes about your early grocery experiences. You certainly have an interesting background, and you have given me the idea of including an independent retailer's story in my next book."

"Thanks for agreeing to meet up, Robbie," John told me with a smile. "I hope I can be of some help."

"I'm sure you can. First of all, why did you leave the Co-op when your apprenticeship ended?"

"I was nineteen years old, and didn't see any immediate prospects of promotion. I'd seen many sales representatives (reps) in smart suits and driving nice cars, and wanted to get out 'on the road' as I thought I could be a successful salesman. I kept asking reps if there were any vacancies, and eventually – after a year – my first chance came to sell biscuits for a company called Associated Biscuits."

"How did that work out, John?"

"Very well. I did that for over four years. It was hard work with a lot of travelling but good money, and I was able to find a job selling cakes for a company which had a good name for quality. After nine successful years, a better opportunity presented itself and I worked for United Biscuits for six years during which time I was promoted twice to become development account negotiator and trainer."

"What did you gain out of all that experience?"

"Confidence, good communication skills, creating trust and building my sales figures – but mainly, by the age of 39, I had matured and was ready for a bigger challenge, and I had the ambition to own and run my own shop."

"Is this the moment you took the plunge to open your own grocery store?" I asked him.

"Yes, but it certainly wasn't a neat Olympic dive with double somersault, with twist and pike. It was a nerve-wracking time. Doreen pledged her help in the enterprise, and with mixed feelings we sold our comfortable home and left our community in Crossford. We were able to purchase a small grocery shop with an upstairs flat in Pittenweem. We encountered problems gaining entry to the flat, and initially we had to sleep in our caravan parked in the street! Our son had to move school from Dollar to Waid, so it was an up-heaval. But luckily Doreen was able to carry on working, and our youngest boy was able to start his primary one year in Pittenweem."

"What were your early days in the business like?"

"The shop premises date back to 1612. It had been run-down with little investment, and opening times were old-fashioned – open at 8am in the morning, closed for one and a half hours for lunch, closed at 5.30pm, and a Wednesday half-day. We immediately altered hours and opened from 8am to 8pm."

"That must have been an immediate help," I observed.

"Sure was. The change of hours alone made us very popular with the locals, and weekly sales grew instantly."

"Did you make any other changes? "

"Yes, to find my feet I ran the store under the Mace group fascia. It was a steep learning curve, but with the wholesaler many miles away I was not getting any benefits of local advertising. After a year I moved to Spar, and things began to pick up. Because of increased sales volumes, we at-tracted better terms from other suppliers. I was gaining confi-dence and cutting costs by carefully altering staff hours of work and staff training."

"Were you eventually able to say you were enjoying the experience?"

"Absolutely," John replied. "Doreen helped out at times that suited, and my job satisfaction soared. I felt everything I had imagined was falling into place."

"So the symbol group helped?"

"Yes, it did... but for reasons I'd rather not go into, I felt compelled to sever my links with the Spar wholesaler, which charged heavily for the service they provided."

"That sounds serious," I remarked.

"It was and it wasn't. I moved to trade with Watson and Philip's Trademarket Cash and Carry Division, and found I could get my main supplies delivered free from the local Kirkcaldy depot. They were operating under the "Day Today" fascia (also supplied free), run by the 'Nisa Today' national buying group, and their own brands sold very well. Trademarkets offered valuable help, with sales advisers calling on me regularly."

As planned, John's wife Doreen arrived at this point. I was quite keen to obtain her views on their step into the 'unknown'. John introduced me, and very soon we were chatting about her impressions on the entry into their brave new world. "Tell me please, Doreen, what do you remember about those very early days in Pittenweem?"

"After we got over the domestic changes in our life, I started getting involved in the shop and actually learned how to use the 'dreaded' till – and how to safely strip down and clean the deli slicing machines," she explained. "I got to know the excellent staff ladies, and the part-time boys and girls who worked with us. We also supplied the local fishing fleet, and my most dangerous moments were when – on Sunday mornings – I, as 'winchman', helped John by lowering boxes of supplies thirty feet down to him, then hanging on to the slippery ladder as I joined him on the deck of a heaving boat."

"So, quite a team effort," I observed.

John spoke up first. "I could never have done it without Doreen's help. Together, we worked on refurbing the shop and extending the back store, and we cooked our own hams which went down very well with the local B&B's and visitors."

"Hard work, but did you have any highlights?"

"Oh, yes! We won 'Scotland's Village Store of the Year' award in 2004, Doreen said gleefully. "A superb accolade to retire with in 2005."

"Don't forget our VIP customer, Doreen!" John prompted her.

"How could I! Yes, one customer – a former Lady in Waiting to the Queen, who lived locally – came in after church one Sunday accompanied by Princess Margaret and a bodyguard. Sadly I didn't see them."

"Oh? Why was that?" I enquired.

"Would you believe, I was in the garden at the time and John – to his everlasting shame – didn't tell me till later, because he thought I was too 'garden scruffy' to be 'presented'!" We all laughed.

"We also won the Spar 'Retailer of the Year'," John said, "and had a fabulous all-expenses-paid two-week holiday in Tenerife."

"Happy days then, you two?"

"We had fifteen glorious years, and only sold because a big supermarket was soon to come rather close," John clarified. "Best of all, we felt we immediately fitted in to the community, and now the youngsters who worked on Saturdays are grown up and have their own wee families. We truly feel that we were exactly what we intended to be: a community convenience shop."

"All hard work, though?"

"We concentrated so much on the shop, we hardly had any time off, so after all the years of running the business we began to enjoy lovely long holidays." I immediately felt the rapport that, like the grocers of old, John and Doreen were proud, upstanding and well-respected individuals in the community.

Just like any 18th century local town or village trader, John and Doreen Mc Gowan felt that urge to be a part of – and serve – the local community. They certainly more than fulfilled the 21st century role of the independent retail grocery store, yet retained the very essence of being the valued 'local grosser'.

CHAPTER 20

"The Demise of the Sales Rep", or "Changing Times in Retail"

RECENTLY, by good fortune, I met John – a long-retired sales rep who, in the 1970s, called regularly to speak with W&P buyers. When I told him I was writing about my early W&P days and would welcome his help in plotting the changes he encountered during his selling career, he kindly agreed to be interviewed.

"It's interesting," John told me, "because over three decades I was part of the huge changes that took place in the grocery trade. Many sales reps not only became redundant, but the occupation of the commercial traveller or sales representative almost entirely disappeared."

"I'd be delighted to get a sales rep's perspective on how and why those changes came about," I explained, keen to know more about this area of the retail world.

"Where do you want me to begin?" he asked.

I considered my answer before speaking. "How about starting off with how you came in to the selling business, in the first place, and take it on from there?"

"I didn't leave school dreaming of being a salesman. I served my time as an engineer but – prior to that – I had been a message boy, just like you, and was aware of sales reps driving around in smart cars. Nearing the end of my engineering apprenticeship, an elderly man I knew had been a salesman with a major biscuit company and passed to me his old sales training manual. It was pure luck – I discovered the theory of how to sell and deal with potential customers. The manual explained everything – the A to Z of selling – and I was fascinated.

"In those days the *Dundee Courier and Advertiser* printed columns of vacancies for sales people, van salesmen and especially reps. I saw a job advertisement for a toothpaste salesperson and I applied. Of course, I was not even 'wet behind the ears' – I had no sales knowledge whatsoever – but I'd swotted the sales manual from end to end and, although I was bereft of any experience, I was able to 'talk the language'. I was thanked for attending the interview, and advised to keep trying."

"Did you feel disheartened?"

"Of course. The job must have been filled, but amazingly I received a letter only a few weeks later telling me that a different vacancy had surprisingly cropped up and would I like to come for an interview? That was my start."

"What year was that," I enquired, "and what was your typical week?"

"That was 1969, and my calls numbered about ten each day," he explained. "Calling on small grocery shops, branches of multiples (such as Wm Low, Galbraiths, Cochranes Templeton), Co-ops, chemist shops in small towns and warehouses in Dundee. On a call cycle of two weeks, I was making sales calls to approximately a hundred customers.

"What plusses did you experience?"

"Of course, the company car – a Ford Prefect, no less – and meeting so many retailers and learning about their business."

"Any minuses?"

"Yes," he said without hesitation: "unproductive time."

"What do you mean?" I asked him.

"There were so many reps 'on the road' in those days, queues of salesmen waiting to speak to the manager formed outside shops. The unwritten rule amongst reps was that we wouldn't leap in and jump the queue; it was no place for the faint-hearted. It was not unheard of to stand waiting for forty minutes for the manager to free himself from serving a long queue of customers."

This certainly sounded like a high-pressure kind of experience. "Can you give me some idea about the orders and deliveries of your product?"

"Sure," he agreed readily. "Orders I received were delivered one week after I called. Minimum orders were ten cases of the product, and best terms were based on fifty cases."

"Did you simply take an order and go on your way?"

"My main responsibility was to secure a sale and see a growth in sales. That meant beating the competition by doing some merchandising, such as making sure my products were being promoted inside the shop. Sometimes I had to set up small displays on stands, which my company provided. I recall I had twenty 'lines' or items on my list of products, and had to try and have each line stocked by my customer."

"So you had a hundred accounts to look after, each offering a maximum of twenty products?"

"That's correct," John confirmed. "It was all carefully controlled by the company. I had to submit a control sheet to my manager showing every product or 'line' was stocked and log what merchandising I did. I got bonus points for growth in sales, but the best bonus I received was for introducing a new line."

"Sounds like a tough world," I remarked.

"Yes, it was a slog, and I began to realise that success depended entirely on the company's ability to develop new products and TV advertising."

"How many years did you spend selling toothpaste?"

"About five years, and then I heard on the 'grapevine' of a vacancy coming up in a paper products company selling to the grocery trade and successfully applied. That proved to be my only employer until I retired," he told me.

"That was quite fortunate."

"It certainly was. It was during all those years I witnessed the many changes which came about."

With so much experience in his role, he must have seen significant developments taking place during his time with the company. "What were the changes, and why do you think they happened?"

"I remember being told that the directors of my company had visited manufacturers in the United States and saw at first hand that reps were spending days 'on the road' but not picking up one order because the smart companies were selling and delivering into central distribution centres. So the writing was on the wall," he explained.

"Were you surprised?"

"Strangely, I had seen for some time signs of inefficiency in the distribution of products to shops, and I used to wonder how long it would take for companies to cut out the waste."

"What waste was that?" I queried.

"I couldn't help seeing what was wasteful. It was simply mathematical. For instance, in the toothpaste world 36 cases of my product could be loaded on to a pallet and only 26 pallets could be loaded on to a covered lorry. With no forklift trucks available at shops to offload goods, only one level of pallets could be loaded. This meant large vehicles, half empty, were driving around delivering 'fresh air'."

"What do you think triggered the changes?"

"Not one single cause – but manufacturers, in the UK, began to realise that rather than send reps out to every retail establishment it was more efficient to have them call on one central point. For example, it was simpler for one rep to call on a symbol group such as a VG or Spar central warehouse and obtain orders. That allowed manufacturers to discuss product promotions with the wholesaler and meant growing business, but it also cleverly left the wholesaler to do the costly distribution to group members. Likewise, rather than have salesmen call in to every branch of a multiple such as Wm Low or Massey, it was more efficient to have one salesman call on the HQ."

"So, that suited everyone?" I prompted him.

"Yes, it did. The very small shops were left out, but they were able to buy in Cash and Carries which were developing in those days."

"Were there any downsides?"

"A few," John confided. "I remember calling at a central distribution depot and found around twenty or thirty reps queueing to speak with buyers. But that soon changed when I was required to start making regular booked appointments with buyers."

"So bulk buying became the norm?"

"Yes," he agreed. "Multiples – especially out-of-town superstores – were growing at the expense of small retailers and symbol groups. Co-ops were merging, and eventually multiples started acquiring smaller multiples. Sales people 'on the road' disappeared. Orders for product are now counted in thousands of cases, and of course the bigger the deals the better the price.

"So what was left?"

"A few senior qualified 'graduate-type' sales executives would work directly with the giant supermarket companies. Today, there will be a new breed of salesperson for every manufacturer calling in to the headquarters of the giant retailers."

This sounded like a costly solution. "Surely every manufacturer can't afford to have a senior person based in London or Manchester, or wherever multiples have their HQ?"

"That's true, but there's another development."

"Ah. What's that, John?"

"Smaller manufacturers now do their selling through agencies," he clarified, "and there are some large agencies which carry out the selling job for dozens of companies.

"It seems like the selling function has changed hugely," I observed.

"I'll say it has. Where there were once hundreds if not thousands of reps within the grocery world, there are now probably only dozens across the UK. Of course, since supermarkets now have scanning at the checkouts, the next orders are automatically computer calculated and sent online to the manufacturer and delivered to the central distribution centre for each supermarket company in the UK. Other computer programmes and e-mailing have also had an impact. The one thing that still happens is that special promotions will be designed and programmed by a promotional team of specialists."

"Would you like to be selling to the grocery trade nowadays?" I asked, curious to hear his response.

"I'd need to be a university graduate dealing with multi-million buying and promotional planning. Even in the 1970s, Proctor and Gamble – the soap detergent producers – were hiring graduates. So 'no' is the answer."

"Progress, John!" I smiled.

"Bigger businesses and clever technology!" he laughed in response.

Hearing John's recollections emphasised to me just how rapid the pace of change had been across so many different aspects of the retail world over those turbulent decades. It seemed to me that no corner of the industry had remained untouched during this tempestuous period of fast-moving developments.

CHAPTER 21

"Did I Make the Right Decision?", or "John Allardice Chat"

ONE of the most amazing and heart-warming moments in my life is that in 2018, at the end of my advertised talk to Friends of Dundee City Library about my first book, *The Grocer's Boy: A Slice of his Life in 1950s Scotland*, a tall gentleman who had sat in the back row approached me.

"That was a very interesting talk, Mr Murray," he said politely. "I've bought the book and can I ask you to sign it for me, please?"

"Yes, thanks. Of course I'll sign..." Then I stopped in my tracks. I recognised the face. It was John Allardice, once my sixteen-year-old apprentice in Willie Low's Logie Street branch... and I had included him in the book! I couldn't believe my luck; I'd given up ever meeting young John. He was a bright, eager young grocer – keen to learn, and a valuable assistant to me.

Since that pleasant surprise I have kept in touch with John, who was able to re-introduce me to John Thomson (now aged 93), another former Willie Low colleague who was my manager for a short time in the Carnoustie branch where I completed my grocery apprenticeship in the 1950s. Imagine the luck of my book helping me to find two long-lost colleagues!

Wm Low & Co. plc was acquired by Tesco in 1994, and John found himself redundant after 31 years of service. John has also now pointed me in the direction of the Facebook page "I Used to Work for Willie Low's", which has opened up for me an insight not only into Wm Low's progress in the UK multiple retail grocery world but the depth of nostalgia I can detect by the comments from employees at every level throughout the company.

My uncertain decision to leave Wm Low in 1963 (a pivotal moment in my life, which I describe in my second *Grocer's Boy* book) to pursue my career in training and education has always left me wondering if I had made the right decision. Discovering John has now opened up a marvellous opportunity for me to hear how his career had developed, how Wm Low operated, and – at the same time – provide me with a sense of what I may have achieved or missed had I remained in the company.

We met in a Dundee coffee shop. "Thanks for joining me to chat about the 'old Willie Low' days," I acknowledged with grateful thanks.

"It's great to meet up with you again, Robbie," John said with a smile.

"As you know, John, I left Low's in 1963 and – instead, at the age of 23, of managing the company's third self-service store in Dundee – I went off into a different world. I know you remained with the company for many years, and I wonder if you would outline how the company grew into one of the biggest and most successful grocery supermarket companies in the UK?"

"Yes, of course, Robbie," he readily replied. "How can I help?"

"First of all, what progress did you make in the company?"

"I'd been a message boy at the Brantwood Avenue store; the first shop you managed before you moved to manage Logie Street branch. That was where I started my apprenticeship. Later I was manager at Arbroath, then Perth Road in Dundee, followed by Berwick and then Kirkcaldy branches before becoming an Area Manager."

"That was brilliant progress," I told him. "When we last worked together in the Logie Street branch in Dundee, the shop was around 700 square feet and was described as self-selection. How did stores change from that period onwards?"

"Stores were never self-selection again; they were either converted to, or built as, new self-service stores."

"What were the approximate square-foot sizes of the stores you managed?" I asked him.

"From what I recall, Arbroath was around 2,000, Perth Road was 4,000, then a leap up to 11,000 at Berwick and then a massive jump to 44,000 at Kirkcaldy."

"Did the stock range change much?"

"Yes, it did. Eventually all stores had delicatessen, butchery, and fruit and veg departments."

"Quite a change in the operation," I remarked. "So, how did staff numbers alter?"

"There was some specialisation, but as an example a 20,000 square foot store would employ about 150 staff – of which only around 30 would be full-time."

"Thinking of the huge Kirkcaldy store, how on earth did you manage to keep the shelves filled?"

"We had to start 'night-filling', where a night manager would supervise a shift from 10pm through to 6am," he explained.

"When I go shopping nowadays, I marvel at the scanning procedure at the checkouts. When was that introduced?"

"It would have been around 1984."

"Did you find that useful?"

"It was more than that – it became essential, because it provided stock reordering information, and helped us to analyse the best and slowest sellers. Equally essential, it made sure every item was priced correctly. Physical stock-takes were still required every thirteen weeks and, in the case of specialised departments, every four weeks."

"Moving on to your days as an area manager, how many stores did you supervise?" I enquired.

"In the early days, before my time, it was around twelve to fifteen branches. But as store sizes increased, I found myself responsible for eight or nine stores."

"And were you responsible for engaging staff?"

"The store manager was allowed to recruit part-time staff, and I was involved when it came to recruiting full-time and the more senior branch positions."

"How about training and personnel duties?"

"Store managers, with or without my help, were required to supervise training and personnel in stores up to about 20,000 square feet, but a personnel manager was employed in stores over that size," he clarified.

Clearly procedures had changed in the period following my departure. "Who was responsible for training and recruitment of managers?" I asked John.

"I was, along with the HQ training and personnel managers."

"What were your biggest concerns?"

"Meeting profit targets. The margins were very tight. Success was measured by how many pence in the pound we made. At a company level, for example, the profit performance ranged from about 2p to about 3p profit for of every £1 of sales."

This was certainly food for thought. "Over the period of your career, John, did you have some high and possibly low moments?"

"Yes, Bob – I'm happy to say I had mainly high moments, such as building my management team, opening a new store, feeling part of the success of the company... and of course the time when I clocked up my 25 years of service."

"Any lows?" I enquired.

"No, there were no lows in Lows!" John smiled. "Except when the end of the company came in 1994."

"On that point, how or why do you think the end of Willie Lows came?"

"We were squeezed in the middle by the giants like Tesco and the smaller supermarket groups, and I think we had reached the highest number of potential store sites we could find."

"What is the state of the retail grocery market situation today?"

"The big four supermarkets are, in descending order: Tesco, Sainsbury, Asda and Morrisons, and they have around 70% of the market," John told me.

"And who has the remaining part?"

"At least 10% or more is held by what are known as the 'discounters' – that's Aldi and Lidl – and the balance by the Co-op, smaller supermarket chains like Booths in England, and of course symbol groups like Costcutter."

"I admire the Co-op for their 'stickability', and especially for taking the decision to support small far-flung communities in the Highlands and Islands," I added.

"Yes, they play an important part in the marketplace. I read recently that they opened the UK's first self-service store in London in 1948. They have always been innovative, but never ventured into giant stores."

"That's amazing," I responded. "They deserve success." I was also interested to find out more about the Willie Low Facebook group. "With your advice I went online to view the Facebook group for former Willie Lows employees, and I pick up a very good vibe from each contributor along with quite a bit of nostalgia. Why do you think the Facebook page is so popular?"

"There's no doubt that there was, and still is, a huge sadness at the loss of our company. Colleagues from all parts and levels of the workforce are so keen to share their memories, jokes, laughs and the nostalgia for all their experiences, even in the finest of detail. People still remember, for example, the scanning codes for certain products," he told me.

"Why do you think the Facebook page is still so popular? After all, the company ceased trading nearly 30 years ago."

"I'm not really surprised; there was a strong company loyalty amongst staff at every level. Everyone took great pride in their work, and there was a work hard, play hard attitude."

"Why was that, John?" I queried.

"It came from the top. Managers were seen to work hard and long hours, and this gained respect. Also, I have to say, we looked after staff regarding pay, conditions and facilities, including the Payment by Results bonuses."

"It certainly comes across as a happy and energetic company to work for," I remarked, remembering my own bygone experiences.

"Absolutely," he readily agreed.

"Just one final point, John. As you know, I've wondered for years whether I did the wrong thing by leaving the company. But as a young manager, I was influenced by a lot of negatives by older managers."

"What do you mean, Bob?"

"With the prospect of moving away from counter service and the control managers had over cash handling and goods-in checks, there were worries about losing profit. Was I right to have had those worries?"

"Yes, in the early days it was almost impossible to control every checkout," John admitted. "You would have had concerns for ten years until scanning was introduced. However, I must admit as stores became much bigger I was always nervous that I was receiving all the correct stock I was being invoiced for. It was better if I could find reliable and trusted people to supervise each area. In the retail trade, there's always worries."

"That's been very helpful, John, and thanks for your time. I certainly feel I missed being part of the success of Wm Low, and yes – perhaps my worries would not have been so bad as I'd imagined."

John had given me a fascinating insight into the role Lows had played in the grocery trade, and I was grateful to him for having shared it with me. It certainly opened my eyes to the ways in which the 'front line' of grocery shopping had continued to change and diversify long after I had made my move into further education and, from there, on to different professional experiences in the world of commerce.

My long-awaited chat with John was over. I had to admire how he had coped in the very demanding role of area manager. After all those intervening hard-working years we had both enjoyed (?), it was a unique opportunity to obtain an insight of the world I could have had. Did I make the right decision? There's no such thing as an easy life in any management role. We each suffered an early retirement: John by the takeover by Tesco in 1994, and me by my real job in Dundee ending in that same year – although I had eight more years in England in a reduced capacity, I too was redundant at the age of 62.

The verdict: perhaps there was not much to choose between the two different routes after all?

CHAPTER 22

"Dundee: A City of Discovery and Influence", or "A Tale of Two Scottish Grocery Giants"

DUNDEE is a remarkable city. I have heard it said many times it is the city of discovery. This, I believe, is on account of its great and everlasting ability to re-invent itself. Possibly its early days as a 'frontline' North Sea whaling port, its linen mills, and later its expanding and worldwide trade in importing and processing jute. Every so often it has risen to the challenge to find economic survival for its inhabitants. Now, in the 21st century and the world of 'high-tech' computer games, it has promoted itself into the new future world landscape. It must have been quite exciting living through the years to witness the changes, even if they didn't bring wealth and riches to every family.

Only recently I have come to realise, in my own small way, I was part of a period in the city's history which has hitherto been given little or no due recognition. Two businesses in the city, not imported but 'homespun', made a mark in their respective spheres. One, in the world of retail grocery, and the other responsible for an impressive impact on wholesale food distribution. Oddly enough, both organisations arrived on the scene quite separately around the late 1880s, both made their greatest impact in the 1980s, and sadly both succumbed to the rigours of competition in the hot bed of the 20th century forces of high-powered finance and trampling growth by giant trading predators.

There are two elements which I'd like to refer to. The first pertains to the striking parallels of each enterprise, and the second, my part within each company which dominated my life and leaves me, to this day, questioning my judgement. The retail grocery business to which I refer is Wm Low & Co. Ltd, and the other the wholesale food distributor Watson & Philip plc. My privilege was to have been a part of both.

The parallels are striking: modest family origins, careful nurturing of the business, and determined ambitions to grow. Steady and secure financial growth, influencing standards, culminating in their greatest moments when they scaled the heights of financial success in the 1980s. They each expanded beyond their geographic boundaries followed by their respective fights to survive, and the tragic end when their influence had gone and their names became history. Distraught employees, left to wonder why it had all gone so badly wrong, now had only their imbued memories deeply rooted in their minds and still wistfully reminisce twenty years later about the impact on their lives and how their memories are never likely to die. Nostalgia, yes – such was the strength of identity, dedication, respect and (yes, I'll say it) the love and admiration each employee had for the business of which they were a part. When a business sets out to nurture and develop company loyalty, the human cost and misery becomes apparent when the organisation sinks. When I think of it, it's rather like a ship's crew: bound together by a badge, standards and discipline, and left to grieve when their beloved vessel sinks.

Although I have no information to cover the entire period for both companies, it is of interest to compare the two businesses over the years:

- **1969**: W&P sales were £12m and profit was £80k
- **1970**: W&P sales were £16m and profit was £280k
- **1973**: W&P sales were £21m and profit was £0.5m; Wm Low sales were £2.5m and profit was £0.5m
- **1981**: Wm Low sales were £108m and profit was £2.2m
- **1984**: Wm Low sales were £154m and profit was £5.7m
- **1993**: W&P sales were £513m and profit was £12.5m; Wm Low sales were £446m and profit was £22m

An amazing likeness, comparing 1973 and 1993. The banks' record takings in Dundee must have experienced a severe drop in 1994!

* * *

The Wm Low story began in 1868, when James Low rented a shop in Hunter Street, Dundee, and began trading as a retail grocer. In 1870 he was joined in the business by his brother William. Meanwhile, James linked with Wm Lindsay to form Lindsay & Low: a company manufacturing preserves, confectionery and bread. Such was the growth in that business, James Low, in 1879, handed over the grocery business to William – and so Wm Low was born. It was a time of great change, when other 'multiple' grocery chains were founded.

Low's was unique in that it was based on the east of Scotland, whereas other notable grocery success stories such as Liptons, Templetons and Galbraiths were based in the Glasgow area and also founded around the late 1880s.

We have learned earlier how, not far from Hunter Street, Bell's Court was the embryonic partnership home of Joseph Philip and Thomas Watson who founded their infant business in 1873 dealing with food imports and food supplies to caterers.

Wm Low's growth was striking and, with 64 branches, by 1900 it became a limited company in 1917. While Watson and Philip's business was successfully developing in the Dundee area, it was not until 1898 that a branch was opened in Aberdeen. It would seem likely that it was relatively easier to expand the number of branches in retail, as presumably both premises and trained employees were more easily found. Finding warehouse premises and the people who understood importing and the wholesale trade was likely to be more difficult. However, it is interesting to note that W&P became a limited company in 1919.

Wm Low's modus operandi was to run on a high turnover, low margin basis, while Watson and Philip found higher margins in its wholesale catering market. The leaders of both businesses made great strides in their respective markets, with Watson and Philip acquiring warehouse premises at Craig Street, near the harbour, and adding branches in Glasgow and Edinburgh. Wm Low, meanwhile, continued adding shops to the group and had moved to larger warehouse premises in Blackness Road, Dundee, and – in time – facilities in Gateshead and Livingston.

Following the Second World War, which had disrupted people in both businesses and slowed down advances in

POSTSCRIPT

SOMETIME in 2005, while I was living in North Devon, word came to me through my family that Eddie had been in touch and was enquiring after my good health and had sent me his 'kind regards'. Upon hearing this I immediately wrote to Eddie and expressed my congratulations on his success. I added that I hoped we could possibly meet when I was next in the area visiting my mother, and expressing my sadness that our 'happy days of yesteryear' had ended for all the wrong reasons.

With little delay I received Eddie's reply in which he also regretted our great relationship had ended, and he invited me to let him know when I would next be in Carnoustie. I met Eddie and his wife Cath on a match day at Tannadice Park, Dundee – the home of Dundee United FC – and enjoyed a lunch with them. Due to his prostate cancer problem Eddie was not entirely well at that point, but he was making every effort to continue conducting his social life and carry out his Dundee United Club responsibilities with a superb, cheerful outlook.

I joined them at home after the game and we reminisced about our happy family get-togethers, the trips we had made on business conferences, and had a good laugh about the many amusing incidents we had shared with friends and colleagues. Despite his bad health and new wealth, Eddie was still the same gregarious charismatic character I'd known. He was a very able businessman, and conveyed a natural down-to-earth demeanour with everyone he came into contact with. Our working relationship was always professional and comfortable. We didn't dwell on his departure from W&P; I sensed we both wanted to put that sad chapter behind us.

Regrettably, I returned to North Devon and, when I heard of his death, I was unable to attend his funeral as I was abroad at the time. It is with great relief that we healed the break in our relationship before he left us.

Upon reading my W&P story, he would have undoubtedly corrected one or two (or more!) of my observations and then probably add something in his characteristic cheeky fashion, like: "Just think how the company could have grown in the 70s and 80s if we'd had a half-decent personnel manager!"

Typical Eddie. Well done you!

ACKNOWLEDGEMENTS

I DEDICATE this story to all of my former fellow employees who worked in Watson and Philip plc and who I was privileged to work with during my 33 years with that great company. Over the years I witnessed at first hand the energy, commitment and positive attitude of everyone – warehouse, drivers and office staff, supervisors, managers and directors I worked with and have learned of their conscientious attitude during the last months, weeks and days when it all seemed lost – and the end came.

When I came back to Carnoustie in 2014 to help look after mum as she approached her one hundredth year, I made time to arrange a W&P reunion. With a brief word in the local newspaper to advertise the gathering in Queen's Hotel in Dundee, perhaps not surprisingly almost a hundred former colleagues appeared. After around twenty years it took time to recognise some faces, but thankfully name badges were at hand. It speaks volumes for the feeling, still beating in the hearts, that so many wanted to meet and chat.

My sincere thanks to my friends and former colleagues for information supplied and access to papers, articles and records:

John Allardice
Graham Bowie
Dennis Charlton
Ian Dutch

Sandy Fyfe
Sheila Gadd
Tom Gallacher
Jimmy Harper
Alistair Jack
Elaine Jewson
John and Doreen McGowan
Murray McGregor
David McPherson Nicol
Mike Rae
Iain Roberts
Calder Sturrock
Ralph Thompson
Steve Wilkie
and
my brother James (Peem) Murray for his sketches.

It is with great sadness that I have to report the death of my old school friend John Blair, alas 'Jock', my rival message boy in the 1950s who featured in my first *Grocer's Boy* book. We were close friends, and shared many interests and memories of 'the good old days'. He will be sadly missed.

* * *

With love and best wishes to my grandchildren Lucy and Jonny Brown and Charlie and Alfie Pugh.

* * *

No criticism of any person alive or dead is intended in the publication of this work.

Original Watson & Philip records, books and artefacts were indexed and stored by Murray McGregor and Robert Murray, and are available for inspection in Dundee City Archives.

REFLECTIONS

L ITTLE did I realise as a twelve-year-old message laddie dashing about the streets and countryside around my home town Carnoustie on my 'big basket' pedal bike that I would spend all my working life in the grocery trade in one capacity or another.

My day release and evening class studies at Dundee Commercial College in the 1950s included product knowledge along with the ancient 'arts' of coffee roasting and tea tasting. Never in my teenage dreams did I expect to see grocery counter service shops eventually replaced by giant superstores offering butchery meat, delicatessen, fruit and vegetables and clothing along with kiosks selling dry cleaning and shoe repair services.

In my thirty years I had experienced cash handling in 'over the counter' service (while unhygienically handling slices of cooked meat and bacon) to witnessing stores so large that the cash handling was done at up to twenty, or more, checkouts. Nor could I have perceived the introduction of computer applications which were capable of registering prices by reading a series of black lines of varying width called a 'barcode' while at the same time logging sales of each category of stock, creating the reordering requirements and keeping check on the profits of all goods in the store.

While I write this in the year 2022, we are already seeing signs that some large retail stores occupying prime high street sites are being forced to close their premises because competitors are selling goods of a similar nature online and delivering direct to customers' homes by van – and, perhaps sooner than we think, by drone. Already we are aware that moving goods and groceries around the country will be done by driverless vehicles.

When we consider that the practice of selling products from shops or stalls had not changed for many centuries, the changes in selling methods in the period from the 1970s to the present day is indeed a staggering revolution – and the future holds even more breathtaking advances which I would love to witness! Or not!

I've been blessed to have spent my entire working life in what I describe the 'golden years'. At no time in the past have people, in the developed world, during that unique period enjoyed almost full lifetime employment, improving living and working conditions, complete with comfortable pensions. It's unlikely such conditions will ever be seen again.

* * *

The River

"...And the river of old grew in volume, bolder and bolder as it swept majestically down the valley, its regime forming such a force that its trickling infancy would not have recognised its power and shape – as it brought great richness and succour to the land and the people living within its sphere – when it reached its most prolific state and entered into a luscious green plain, its influence was at its greatest – its role in nature complete and its future secure – until one day without warning a tsunami from an unknown source so powerful that it devastated the river and all the goodness around she had provided – so the river was no more, and those who had lived along its banks were left only with the memories and images of a once-great, benevolent friend of the valley..."

Anon.

ILLUSTRATIONS

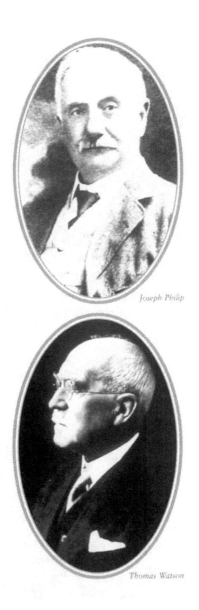

Joseph Philip

Thomas Watson

Joseph Philip and Thomas Watson,
the founders of Watson and Philip

The Watson and Philip plc board of directors, early 1970s,
showing (left to right), Iain Philip, Herbert Philip, Frank Philip
(back row), Harry Gardner, J.B. Thomson (front row).

Me presenting Mr Hugh Strain, aged 100, with an engraved
Caithness Glass centenary goblet.

VAT conference in Dundee in 1973, with me (far left) standing
next to operations manager Eddie Thompson.

Eddie Thompson (second from left) and J.B. Thomson (second
from right) attending a VG conference in the early seventies.

VG retailers and staff head for the tenth anniversary VG
conference in Amsterdam.

A group of cash and carry managers, with director Frank
Keaney (third from left) and J.B. Thomson (second from right).

River Tay raft race, featuring a VG team including Iain Philip (back left) with son Charles Philip (middle second left), Iain Roberts (middle third left).

Jim Harper (far left), VG sales manager, with a VG-sponsored junior football team.

Attending the VG national golf competition, held at St Pierre Golf Club, Chepstow. Left to right: Robert Murray, Harry Lawson (VG retailer, Broughty Ferry), and Ron Beatt (VG retailer, Newport on Tay).

WATSON & PHILIP LTD

TELEPHONE
0382 21411

TELEGRAMS
WATPHIL DUNDEE

DIRECTORS
H. D. PHILIP (CHAIRMAN)
H. S. GARDNER (MANAGING)
J. C. HADDEN   J. MAGILL
L. L. PHILIP   J. G. R. PHILIP
J. Y. PHILIP   J. B. THOMSON

WHOLESALE   FOOD   DISTRIBUTORS

REGISTERED IN SCOTLAND   REGISTRATION No. 1095   REGISTERED OFFICE BLACKNESS BUILDINGS, DUNDEE, DD1 9PU

YOUR REF

OUR REF   ET/AMcG

R. T. Murray, Esq.

Personal

Dear Bob,

Salary Review – June 1975

P.O. BOX 89.
BLACKNESS ROAD
DUNDEE DD1 9PU

17th June, 1975

NEWS BULLETIN of the

Delivered Grocery Division

WATSON & PHILIP LTD
P O Box 89 Blackness Road Dundee

FOODSERVICE

STAFF HANDBOOK

A collection of Watson and Philip letterheads and corporate materials.

Some Watson and Philip branded items:
a model lorry and VG golf ball. From the private collection of
Dennis Charlton.

Some of the Watson and Philip transport fleet and drivers.
Foreground: Douglas Knight (distribution manager). Background (left to right): Bob McBean, Charlie Lawrence, Alex
MacPherson and Ian Osborne (drivers). Photo from the private
archive of Iain Roberts and reproduced by permission.

ABOUT THE AUTHOR

Robert Taylor Murray was born in Barry, near Carnoustie, in 1940. Growing up in Westhaven and later residing in Carnoustie itself, he attended Barry and Carnoustie Schools before becoming an apprentice grocer with William Low & Company Ltd. He qualified as a Member of The Grocers' Institute, and was appointed manager of William Low's Brantwood branch in Dundee, becoming the company's youngest ever manager at the age of 19. He later oversaw the Logie Street branch in Lochee.

Robert went on to manage a larger third branch in Dundee and then, after attending further education management courses, discovered he was sufficiently qualified to successfully apply for a post as a lecturer in distributive trades subjects at Dundee Commercial College – a position he held for five years. Realising how much the retail trade was changing and feeling he was less in touch to reflect the current scene, he applied to join The Grocers' Institute and was appointed Training Development Officer for part of London and east England, where he advised companies and colleges on training in the retail grocery trade.

After two years he returned to the Dundee area when he was appointed Training Officer for Watson & Philip, a national wholesale food distributor. He remained with that company for thirty-three years, during which time he was appointed Personnel Manager and eventually became Group Personnel Manager with responsibility for three thousand employees and, latterly, in the London area.

Robbie's recollections of his early days in the grocery trade, *The Grocer's Boy*, was published by Extremis Publishing in 2018. The story continued in *The Grocer's Boy Rides Again*, published in 2020, which followed Robbie's professional development throughout the busy days and radical changes of the Swinging Sixties.

Following a company acquisition he became redundant at the age of sixty-two. In retirement he has again been actively involved in amateur theatre. He is a member of Tay Writers – a Dundee based writing group – and Angus Writers' Circle, and writes short stories.

He has written a stage presentation on the life of Robert Burns, *The Spirit of Robbie Burns*, which has been performed several times by amateurs in Tayside. The script was published by Extremis Publishing in 2019.